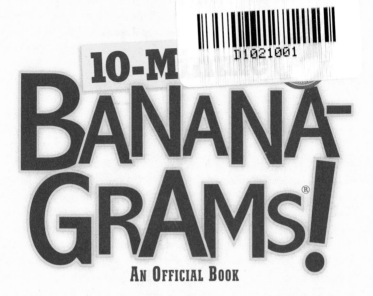

10-MINUTE BANANA-GRAMS®!

AN OFFICIAL BOOK

BY JOE EDLEY

AND
THE CREATORS
OF

BANANAGRAMS®

WORKMAN PUBLISHING • NEW YORK

In memory of Abe Nathanson,
who will always be our Top Banana.

. . . .

Library of Congress Cataloging-in-Publication Data is available

ISBN 978-0-7611-6086-1

Workman books are available at special discounts when purchased in bulk for premiums and sales promotions as well as for fund-raising or educational use. Special editions or book excerpts also can be created to specification. For details, contact the Special Sales Director at the address below, or send an e-mail to specialmarkets@workman.com.

Design by Rae Ann Spitzenberger

Bananagrams® is a trademark owned by Abe Nathanson doing business as Bananagrams, registered U.S. Patent and Trademark Office.

Banana Stopwatch Illustration © pinchukv
Photo © Olga Shelego

WORKMAN PUBLISHING COMPANY, INC.
225 Varick Street
New York, NY 10014-4381
www.workman.com

Printed in the United States of America
First printing September 2010

10 9 8 7 6 5 4 3 2 1

10-Minute WELCOME TO BANANAGRAMS

THE STORY OF BANANAGRAMS

People everywhere have fallen for **Bananagrams,** the addictive craze that started as a simple idea: "An **anagram** game that is so fast it will drive you **bananas**!" And why not? It's amazingly fun and easy to play—you pick lettered tiles and create a grid of connecting and intersecting words as fast as you can.

It all began one summer when three generations of our family were vacationing together on the beach. We wanted a game that everybody—no matter their age—could enjoy. After marathon sessions playing and experimenting with various permutations of word games, we ended up inventing Bananagrams. Our family was hooked—and so we decided to share our new creation with everyone. The next thing we knew the game was named Game of the Year. Not bad for a rainy-day invention.

We took it to the next level with *Bananagrams! The Official Book* and then *More Bananagrams!* Now we're very excited to present *10-Minute Bananagrams!* Loaded with hundreds of new puzzles, this book promises challenges which are extra fast and extra fun. Each puzzle is a perfect portable dose of brain-twisting wordplay—and they can all be solved in 10 minutes or less.

We've continued our collaboration with Joe Edley, who is both a master Bananagrammer and the only three-time National Scrabble Champion in history. He's carefully crafted these smart and fast puzzles, which will thrill solvers of all stripes. So even if you've never grabbed a tile from a Bananagrams pouch, you're sure to find these puzzles very a-*peel*-ing!

HOW TO PLAY

Like the game, the puzzles in *10-Minute Bananagrams!* are super fast and super fun. In all, there are 12 puzzle categories—some offer one big challenge, while others feature a group of shorter problems to solve. There are two levels of difficulty. The half-banana, which is a great entry level for beginners, and the one banana, which are a bit harder to crack. Dive in wherever you feel comfortable. If you're a beginner, you might want to try solving the puzzles with a pencil, because you may need to cross off tiles more than once. But if you're feeling brave, grab a pen!

All of the puzzles can be solved using common English words that appear in any standard dictionary. We've included a list of **Weords** (weird words!) on the facing page which we've compiled especially for Bananagrams players. This list features fun and unusual words that can come in very handy when you get stuck solving a puzzle. Oh, and just for fun, you'll find a list of popular rules variations on page 10 for those who are looking for new and clever ways to play Bananagrams, the game. Flip to the back of the book for the answer key that starts on page 274.

We hope you'll dive right in and start solving. Have fun and don't be surprised if these puzzles drive you bananas!

The Nathanson Family
Creators of Bananagrams

WEORDS!

These **WEORDS** (weird words!) are strange and useful words that can help you be a better Bananagrammer. Have a bunch full of Ⓐs and Ⓞs and Ⓤs? Or maybe you need the perfect 3-letter word that starts with Ⓨ to finish your grid? These lists of handy and unusual words can help get you out of many a Bananagrams jam!

2-LETTER WORDS

AA	AY	ES	IT	NE	OY	UP
AB	BA	ET	JO	NO	PA	US
AD	BE	EX	KA	NU	PE	UT
AE	BI	FA	KI	OD	PI	WE
AG	BO	FE	LA	OE	QI	WO
AH	BY	GO	LI	OF	RE	XI
AI	DE	HA	LO	OH	SH	XU
AL	DO	HE	MA	OI	SI	YA
AM	ED	HI	ME	OM	SO	YE
AN	EF	HM	MI	ON	TA	YO
AR	EH	HO	MM	OP	TI	ZA
AS	EL	ID	MO	OR	TO	
AT	EM	IF	MU	OS	UH	
AW	EN	IN	MY	OW	UM	
AX	ER	IS	NA	OX	UN	

3-LETTER WORDS

AAH	ACT	AGA	AID	ALA	AMA	ANI
AAL	ADD	AGE	AIL	ALB	AMI	ANT
AAS	ADO	AGO	AIM	ALE	AMP	ANY
ABA	ADS	AGS	AIN	ALL	AMU	APE
ABS	ADZ	AHA	AIR	ALP	ANA	APO
ABY	AFF	AHI	AIS	ALS	AND	APP
ACE	AFT	AHS	AIT	ALT	ANE	APT

ARB	BED	BUY	CUP	DOM	EMS	FIB
ARC	BEE	BYE	CUR	DON	EMU	FID
ARE	BEG	BYS	CUT	DOR	END	FIE
ARF	BEL	CAB	CWM	DOS	ENG	FIG
ARK	BEN	CAD	DAB	DOT	ENS	FIL
ARM	BES	CAM	DAD	DOW	EON	FIN
ARS	BET	CAN	DAG	DRY	ERA	FIR
ART	BEY	CAP	DAH	DUB	ERE	FIT
ASH	BIB	CAR	DAK	DUD	ERG	FIX
ASK	BID	CAT	DAL	DUE	ERN	FIZ
ASP	BIG	CAW	DAM	DUG	ERR	FLU
ASS	BIN	CAY	DAN	DUH	ERS	FLY
ATE	BIO	CEE	DAP	DUN	ESS	FOB
ATT	BIS	CEL	DAW	DUO	ETA	FOE
AUK	BIT	CEP	DAY	DUP	ETH	FOG
AVA	BIZ	CHI	DEB	DYE	EVE	FOH
AVE	BOA	CIG	DEE	EAR	EWE	FON
AVO	BOB	CIS	DEF	EAT	EYE	FOP
AWA	BOD	COB	DEL	EAU	FAB	FOR
AWE	BOG	COD	DEN	EBB	FAD	FOU
AWL	BOO	COG	DEV	ECU	FAN	FOX
AWN	BOP	COL	DEW	EDH	FAR	FOY
AXE	BOS	CON	DEX	EDS	FAS	FRO
AYE	BOT	COO	DEY	EEK	FAT	FRY
AYS	BOW	COP	DIB	EEL	FAX	FUB
AZO	BOX	COR	DID	EFF	FAY	FUD
BAA	BOY	COS	DIE	EFS	FED	FUG
BAD	BRA	COT	DIF	EFT	FEE	FUN
BAG	BRO	COW	DIG	EGG	FEH	FUR
BAH	BRR	COX	DIM	EGO	FEM	GAB
BAL	BUB	COY	DIN	EKE	FEN	GAD
BAM	BUD	COZ	DIP	ELD	FER	GAE
BAN	BUG	CRU	DIS	ELF	FES	GAG
BAP	BUM	CRY	DIT	ELK	FET	GAL
BAR	BUN	CUB	DOC	ELL	FEU	GAM
BAS	BUR	CUD	DOE	ELM	FEW	GAN
BAT	BUS	CUE	DOG	ELS	FEY	GAP
BAY	BUT	CUM	DOL	EME	FEZ	GAR

Did You Know?

• The Africans are credited with giving the banana its name. Over the centuries it had been known by many names: *banna*, *Ghana*, and even *funana*.

• In Europe during the 15th and 16th centuries, the banana was known as the "Indian fig."

• In India, bananas were called "Fruit of the Wise Men" because men would meditate under the shady leaves of banana plants.

HOT	JEE	KOA
HOW	JET	KOB
HOY	JEU	KOI
HUB	JEW	KOP
HUE	JIB	KOR
HUG	JIG	KOS
HUH	JIN	KUE
HUM	JOB	KYE
HUN	JOE	LAB
HUP	JOG	LAC
HUT	JOT	LAD
HYP	JOW	LAG
ICE	JOY	LAM
ICH	JUG	LAP
ICK	JUN	LAR
ICY	JUS	LAS
IDS	JUT	LAT
IFF	KAB	LAV
IFS	KAE	LAW
IGG	KAF	LAX
ILK	KAS	LAY
ILL	KAT	LEA
IMP	KAY	LED
INK	KEA	LEE
INN	KEF	LEG
INS	KEG	LEI
ION	KEN	LEK
IRE	KEP	LES
IRK	KEX	LET
ISM	KEY	LEU
ITS	KHI	LEV
IVY	KID	LEX
JAB	KIF	LEY
JAG	KIN	LIB
JAM	KIP	LID
JAR	KIR	LIE
JAW	KIS	LIN
JAY	KIT	LIP

GAS	GNU	HAE	HEW
GAT	GOA	HAG	HEX
GAY	GOB	HAH	HEY
GED	GOD	HAJ	HIC
GEE	GOO	HAM	HID
GEL	GOR	HAO	HIE
GEM	GOS	HAP	HIM
GEN	GOT	HAS	HIN
GET	GOX	HAT	HIP
GEY	GUL	HAW	HIS
GHI	GUM	HAY	HIT
GIB	GUN	HEH	HMM
GID	GUT	HEM	HOB
GIE	GUV	HEN	HOD
GIG	GUY	HEP	HOE
GIN	GYM	HER	HOG
GIP	GYP	HES	HON
GIT	HAD	HET	HOP

LIS	MIL	NET	OHM	OPS	OXO	PEA
LIT	MIM	NEW	OHO	OPT	OXY	PEC
LOB	MIR	NIB	OHS	ORA	PAC	PED
LOG	MIS	NIL	OIL	ORB	PAD	PEE
LOO	MIX	NIM	OKA	ORC	PAH	PEG
LOP	MOA	NIP	OKE	ORE	PAL	PEH
LOT	MOB	NIT	OLD	ORS	PAM	PEN
LOW	MOC	NIX	OLE	OSE	PAN	PEP
LOX	MOD	NOB	OMS	OUD	PAP	PER
LUG	MOG	NOD	ONE	OUR	PAR	PES
LUM	MOL	NOG	ONO	OUT	PAS	PET
LUV	MOM	NOH	ONS	OVA	PAT	PEW
LUX	MON	NOM	OOH	OWE	PAW	PHI
LYE	MOO	NOO	OOT	OWL	PAX	PHT
MAC	MOP	NOR	OPE	OWN	PAY	PIA
MAD	MOR	NOS				
MAE	MOS	NOT				
MAG	MOT	NOW				
MAN	MOW	NTH				
MAP	MUD	NUB				
MAR	MUG	NUN				
MAS	MUM	NUS				
MAT	MUN	NUT				
MAW	MUS	OAF				
MAX	MUT	OAK				
MAY	MYC	OAR				
MED	NAB	OAT				
MEG	NAE	OBA				
MEL	NAG	OBE				
MEM	NAH	OBI				
MEN	NAM	OCA				
MET	NAN	ODA				
MEW	NAP	ODD				
MHO	NAW	ODE				
MIB	NAY	ODS				
MIC	NEB	OES				
MID	NEE	OFF				
MIG	NEG	OFT				

Did You Know?

• In the Pacific Islands, banana leaves are used to treat burns.

• In Latin, Caribbean, and Asian cultures, banana leaves are used as wrappers to steam food.

• If an unripe banana is placed next to a ripe banana, the unripened one will ripen more quickly.

• Banana peels are very versatile. They can be used to do everything from polishing leather shoes to killing warts.

• Banana peels are edible— though not very tasty unless they're cooked.

PIC	RAD	ROE	SHY	TAB	TON	VAR
PIE	RAG	ROM	SIB	TAD	TOO	VAS
PIG	RAH	ROT	SIC	TAE	TOP	VAT
PIN	RAI	ROW	SIM	TAG	TOR	VAU
PIP	RAJ	RUB	SIN	TAJ	TOT	VAV
PIS	RAM	RUE	SIP	TAM	TOW	VAW
PIT	RAN	RUG	SIR	TAN	TOY	VEE
PIU	RAP	RUM	SIS	TAO	TRY	VEG
PIX	RAS	RUN	SIT	TAP	TSK	VET
PLY	RAT	RUT	SIX	TAR	TUB	VEX
POD	RAW	RYA	SKA	TAS	TUG	VIA
POH	RAX	RYE	SKI	TAT	TUI	VID
POI	RAY	SAB	SKY	TAU	TUN	VIE
POL	REB	SAC	SLY	TAV	TUP	VIG
POO	REC	SAD	SOB	TAW	TUT	VIM
POP	RED	SAE	SOD	TAX	TUX	VIS
POT	REE	SAG	SOL	TEA	TWA	VOE
POW	REF	SAL	SOM	TED	TWO	VOW
POX	REG	SAP	SON	TEE	TYE	VOX
PRO	REI	SAT	SOP	TEG	UDO	VUG
PRY	REM	SAU	SOS	TEL	UGH	VUM
PSI	REP	SAW	SOT	TEN	UKE	WAB
PST	RES	SAX	SOU	TET	ULU	WAD
PUB	RET	SAY	SOW	TEW	UMM	WAE
PUD	REV	SEA	SOX	THE	UMP	WAG
PUG	REX	SEC	SOY	THO	UNS	WAN
PUL	RHO	SEE	SPA	THY	UPO	WAP
PUN	RIA	SEG	SPY	TIC	UPS	WAR
PUP	RIB	SEI	SRI	TIE	URB	WAS
PUR	RID	SEL	STY	TIL	URD	WAT
PUS	RIF	SEN	SUB	TIN	URN	WAW
PUT	RIG	SER	SUE	TIP	URP	WAX
PYA	RIM	SET	SUK	TIS	USE	WAY
PYE	RIN	SEW	SUM	TIT	UTA	WEB
PYX	RIP	SEX	SUN	TOD	UTE	WED
QAT	ROB	SHA	SUP	TOE	UTS	WEE
QIS	ROC	SHE	SUQ	TOG	VAC	WEN
QUA	ROD	SHH	SYN	TOM	VAN	WET

WHA	WOK	WYN	YAY	YIP	YUM	ZEP
WHO	WON	XIS	YEA	YOB	YUP	ZIG
WHY	WOO	YAG	YEH	YOD	ZAG	ZIN
WIG	WOS	YAH	YEN	YOK	ZAP	ZIP
WIN	WOT	YAK	YEP	YOM	ZAS	ZIT
WIS	WOW	YAM	YES	YON	ZAX	ZOA
WIT	WRY	YAP	YET	YOU	ZED	ZOO
WIZ	WUD	YAR	YEW	YOW	ZEE	ZUZ
WOE	WYE	YAW	YIN	YUK	ZEK	ZZZ

WORDS WITH A LOT OF VOWELS

AA	AUDIO	LOUIE	OIDIA	ROUE
AALII	AURA	LUAU	OLEA	TOEA
ADIEU	AURAE	MEOU	OLEO	UNAI
AE	AUREI	MIAOU	OLIO	UNAU
AECIA	AUTO	MOUE	OORIE	URAEI
AEON	AWEE	OBIA	OOZE	UREA
AERIE	BEAU	OBOE	OURIE	UVEA
AERO	CIAO	OE	OUZO	ZOEA
AGEE	EASE	OGEE	QUAI	ZOEAE
AGIO	EAU	OI	QUEUE	
AGUE	EAUX			
AI	EAVE			
AIDE	EERIE			
AIOLI	EIDE			
AJEE	EMEU			
AKEE	EPEE			
ALAE	ETUI			
ALEE	EURO			
ALOE	IDEA			
AMIA	ILEA			
AMIE	ILIA			
ANOA	INIA			
AQUA	IOTA			
AREA	IXIA			
ARIA	JIAO			
ASEA	LIEU			

Did You Know?

• Eating bananas between meals is a good, healthy way to keep your blood sugar levels up.

• Bananas are high in iron and can help cure cases of anemia.

• One study showed that 200 students at a British school improved their exam scores by eating bananas at breakfast and lunch.

WORDS WITH NO VOWELS

BRR	HMM	RHYTHM(S)	SYPH(S)
BY(S)	HYMN(S)	RYND(S)	SYZYGY
CRWTH	HYP(S)	SCRY	THY
CRY	LYMPH(S)	SH	THYMY
CRYPT(S)	LYNCH	SHY	TRY
CWM	LYNX	SHYLY	TRYST(S)
CYST(S)	MM	SKY	TSK
DRY(S)	MY	SLY	TYPP(S)
DRYLY	MYC(S)	SLYLY	TYPY
FLY	MYRRH(S)	SPRY	WHY(S)
FLYBY(S)	MYTH(S)	SPRYLY	WRY
FLYSCH	MYTHY	SPY	WRYLY
FRY	NTH	STY	WYCH
GHYLL(S)	NYMPH(S)	STYMY	WYN(S)
GLYCYL(S)	PLY	SYLPH(S)	WYND(S)
GLYPH(S)	PRY	SYLPHY	WYNN(S)
GYM(S)	PST	SYN	XYLYL(S)
GYP(S)	PSYCH(S)	SYNC(S)	XYST(S)
GYPSY	PYGMY	SYNCH(S)	ZZZ
HM	PYX	SYNTH(S)	

Q WORDS WITH NO U

FAQIR(S)	QANAT(S)	QIS
MBAQANGA(S)	QAT(S)	QOPH(S)
QABALA(S)	QI	QWERTY(S)
QABALAH(S)	QINDAR(S)	SHEQALIM
QADI(S)	QINDARKA	SHEQEL(S)
QAID(S)	QINTAR(S)	TRANQ(S)

OTHER WAYS TO PLAY

For all of you who've mastered the basic Bananagrams game and are itching for new ways to play, we're including some popular variations of the game that will help hone your Bananagramming skills.

BANANA SMOOTHIE

To play this less hectic version of the game, place all of the tiles facedown and divide them equally among the players. Play the game as you normally would, except instead of peeling or dumping, each player uses only the tiles they've been given. The first player to use up all of their letters says "Bananas!" and is the winner. If the game ends in a stalemate, the player with the fewest remaining tiles wins.

BANANA SOLITAIRE

To play the game by yourself, place all of the tiles facedown on the table. Take 21 tiles and play the game as you normally would. Only peel when you've used up your existing tiles. See how long it takes you to use up all 144 tiles, and then try to beat your own best time. Or challenge yourself by trying to make as few words as you can with all 144 letters.

BANANA NUMBERS

In this version, all of the rules of the regular game apply. However, instead of using any words they can, players must use a certain number of words or words that are of a certain length. For instance, you could say that each player can only have four words in their grid or only use words that are four letters long. The longer the words or the fewer words allowed in a grid, the harder the game.

BANANA THEMES

Play the game as you normally would, but instead of using any words they can, players must include in their grid at least one word related to a given theme. To make this even more challenging, require players to use two or three (or more!) themed words. Here are some fun ideas for themes: Names of family members, friends, famous people; objects in the room; holiday words; animals; sports; clothing; winter, spring, summer, or fall words; buildings; parts of the body; school; politics; nature; words related to a specific movie, TV show, or book.

BEST BANANA

Divide the tiles evenly among all players. Then, instead of making word grids, have each player try to spell the longest word they can using the tiles they have. Instead of finding the longest word, you can make this a contest to spell the most words, the most unusual words, or even the all-around best words (though judging these can often turn into quite a battle!).

BANANAS ON BOARD

Play the game as you normally would, except limit the sprawl of the word grids. For instance, you could say that each player's grid must fit into a 10×10 tile space or you could rip out sheets of notepaper and use them as "boards." This forces a more condensed playing area and makes the game more challenging.

BANANA CLUES

Play the game as you normally would. At the end, have each player write out a clue for every word that appears in their finished grid. Then everyone passes their clue sheet and their bunch of mixed-up tiles to the player on their right. Using the tiles and clue sheet that were passed to them, each player must try to re-create the grid that the original player formed.

HALF
BANANA

PUZZLES

Rearrange the letters of each word below and place them in the blanks so that, together with the two letters that have already been placed, they form a new word.

PRIM

A _ _ _ T

CARE

P _ _ _ H

PEAR

C _ _ _ T

DEAN

E _ _ _ R

BANANA FILLING

Add an S to each of the words below and then rearrange the letters in each word to form a new six-letter word.

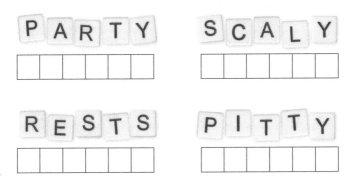

P A R T Y

S C A L Y

R E S T S

P I T T Y

Using three of the tiles from the bunch on the left, fill in the blanks on the right to make a six-letter word that connects the grid.

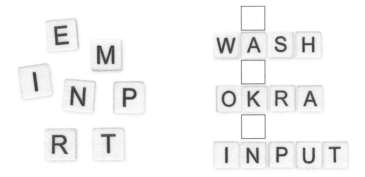

E M
I N P
R T

W A S H
O K R A
I N P U T

BANANA SHAKES

Each of the following six-letter sets can be rearranged to spell out a common word that either starts with BL, EN, or RE or ends with OR, ST, or OW. Find all the words as quickly as you can.

CESTTU
☐☐☐☐☐☐

BENORR
☐☐☐☐☐☐

ALOPRR
☐☐☐☐☐☐

BEHILT
☐☐☐☐☐☐

AGLMOR
☐☐☐☐☐☐

CDEERU
☐☐☐☐☐☐

BORSTU
☐☐☐☐☐☐

BEOSTW
☐☐☐☐☐☐

EEGINN
☐☐☐☐☐☐

ELLOWY
☐☐☐☐☐☐

EIMNTY
☐☐☐☐☐☐

BLOPUW
☐☐☐☐☐☐

16

BANANA PEELS

There is <u>one letter</u> that when added to all of the four-letter words below can be used to form new five-letter words. Find the letter that works for all four words, add it to each word, and then rearrange each set of letters to form a new word. For example, B can be added to LOSS, ONLY, AUTO and IRON to form SLOBS, NOBLY, ABOUT and ROBIN.

COMMON
LETTER

P I L E

P I E R

R U L E

D I T S

BANANARAMA

Each of the words below can be turned into another word on the list by changing one letter and then rearranging them all to form a new word. For example, REGIMENT can be turned into STEERING by changing the M to an S, so they would be a pair. How quickly can you find all the pairs?

Pairs

1. H A Z A R D _ _
2. E D G I L Y _ _
3. C A R B O Y _ _
4. A N I M U S _ _
5. D H A R M A _ _
6. I N D U C E
7. C E L E R Y
8. M I D L E G
9. S I M I A N
10. C R E O L E
11. C Y B O R G
12. F E C U N D

BANANA CHIPS

Each set of letters below is arranged alphabetically, and the ? is in the correct alphabetical position. Figure out what letter the ? represents and rearrange the letters to spell a six-letter word. For example, in A?ENTV the ? could be an A, B, C, D or E. Here it represents a D, which can be combined with the other letters to spell ADVENT. The first letter is placed to get you started.

E E ? L W Y
W ⬜ ⬜ ⬜ ⬜ ⬜

F F I S U ?
S ⬜ ⬜ ⬜ ⬜ ⬜

H I I ? T W
W ⬜ ⬜ ⬜ ⬜ ⬜

A A L S W ?
A ⬜ ⬜ ⬜ ⬜ ⬜

E G I L P ?
P ⬜ ⬜ ⬜ ⬜ ⬜

E E ? L M U
L ⬜ ⬜ ⬜ ⬜ ⬜

B C E H ? U
C ⬜ ⬜ ⬜ ⬜ ⬜

A L N ? U W
W ⬜ ⬜ ⬜ ⬜ ⬜

D E ? M O Y
M ⬜ ⬜ ⬜ ⬜ ⬜

B C E E M ?
B ⬜ ⬜ ⬜ ⬜ ⬜

19

For each bunch below, rearrange the letters to form two intersecting words that fit into the corresponding grid.

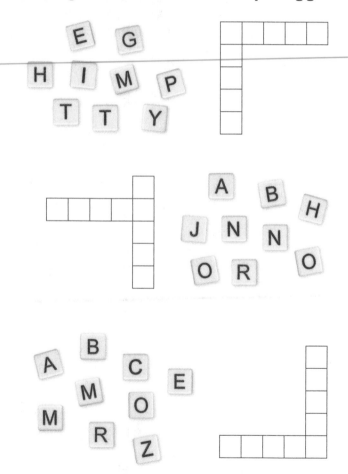

BANANA CRUNCH

Each set of 10 tiles below contains two common five-letter words. The letters of the first five-letter word are adjacent, but not in order. Find them and rearrange them to spell a word. Cross out those letters and imagine that the five remaining letters are now consecutive. These remaining letters can now be rearranged to spell the second word.

Example: GTIAKLPOTH. AKLPO can be rearranged into POLKA. That leaves GTITH, which can be rearranged into TIGHT.

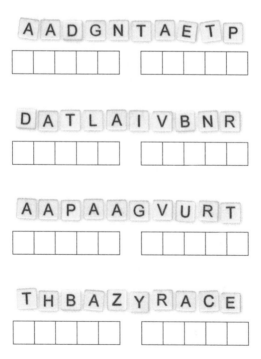

A A D G N T A E T P

D A T L A I V B N R

A A P A A G V U R T

T H B A Z Y R A C E

BANANA PUDDING

Each of the two-letter groups below may be extended both on the right and the left to form a six-letter word. Drawing from the tiles directly above each group, fill in the blanks to find the words as quickly as you can.

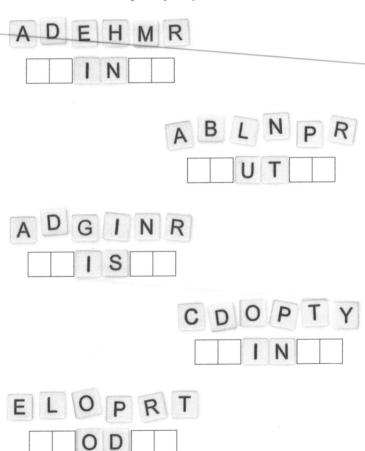

A D E H M R

☐ ☐ I N ☐ ☐

A B L N P R

☐ ☐ U T ☐ ☐

A D G I N R

☐ ☐ I S ☐ ☐

C D O P T Y

☐ ☐ I N ☐ ☐

E L O P R T

☐ ☐ O D ☐ ☐

TOTALLY BANANAS

For each of the words below, replace one letter with the tile after the plus sign. Then rearrange the letters to form something found in a car.

S H A P E D + L

☐☐☐☐☐☐

B A A I N G + R

☐☐☐☐☐☐

B E N I G N + E

☐☐☐☐☐☐

B O A R D + I

☐☐☐☐☐

P R O M O T E D + E

☐☐☐☐☐☐☐☐

A L E R T E S T + B

☐☐☐☐☐☐☐☐

BANANA TREES

Use the 15 tiles in this bunch to create words that fit into the grids below. To get you started, a few tiles from the bunch have been placed in the grid. The BANANA BITES provide hints to help you solve each grid. Reuse the 15 tiles in the bunch for each grid.

Tiles: U B O E I L M N E P P R T T A

1. BANANA BITE: One word is a type of performance.

2. BANANA BITE: One word is a color.

3. BANANA BITE: One word means "fall down."

4. BANANA BITE: One word is someone who fixes pipes.

BUNCH OF BANANAS

For each word or phrase below, rearrange the letters to spell two things that are green. For example, AGILE LOCO CRAB can be rearranged to spell BROCCOLI, ALGAE. The first letter of each word is placed to get you started.

SLAIN   VOWEL
O _ _ _ _   L _ _ _

STEEPLE   RAP
A _ _ _ _ _   T _ _ _

NOSEY   GAME
M _ _ _ _   S _ _ _

CREEPY   SEAL
C _ _ _ _ _   P _ _ _

SMELL   DOVE
M _ _ _   E _ _ _ _

PINK   CHAPELS
S _ _ _ _ _ _   K _ _ _

BANANA BITES

Rearrange the letters of each word below and place them in the blanks so that, together with the two letters that have already been placed, they form a new word.

BEER
H _ _ _ Y

AIRS
D _ _ _ M

DEAR
G _ _ _ N

CANE
D _ _ _ R

BANANA FILLING

Add an R to each of the words below and then rearrange the letters in each word to form a new six-letter word.

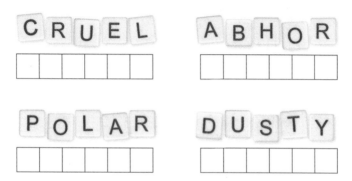

C R U E L

A B H O R

P O L A R

D U S T Y

Using three of the tiles from the bunch on the left, fill in the blanks on the right to make a six-letter word that connects the grid.

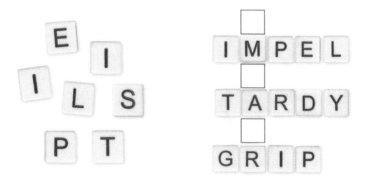

E
I
I
L S
P T

I M P E L

T A R D Y

G R I P

BANANA SHAKES

Each of the following six-letter sets can be rearranged to spell out a common word that either starts with FL, GL, or CL or ends with NG, ME, or LE. Find all the words as quickly as you can.

C G H I L T

B C E E M O

E F L N T U

E E G L N T

A C G I N V

E E G L M U

B E F I L O

G I I N P W

C E L O S T

A C E L S U

A C E G L N

A F L L O R

BANANA PEELS

There is <u>one letter</u> that when added to all of the four-letter words below can be used to form new five-letter words. Find the letter that works for all four words, add it to each word, and then rearrange each set of letters to form a new word. For example, B can be added to LOSS, ONLY, AUTO and IRON to form SLOBS, NOBLY, ABOUT and ROBIN.

COMMON
LETTER

A L T O

B U R Y

O U C H

R U D E

BANANARAMA

Each of the words below can be turned into another word on the list by changing one letter and then rearranging them all to form a new word. For example, REGIMENT can be turned into STEERING by changing the M to an S, so they would be a pair. How quickly can you find all the pairs?

Pairs

1. I C E M E N

___ ___

2. A U B U R N

___ ___

3. M A R O O N

— —

4. E Y E L E T

— —

5. E N I G M A

— —

6. U N M A S K

7. B E E T L E

8. E R M I N E

9. T U R B A N

10. G U I N E A

11. S K Y M A N

12. A M M O N O

30

BANANA CHIPS

Each set of letters below is arranged alphabetically, and the ? is in the correct alphabetical position. Figure out what letter the ? represents and rearrange the letters to spell a six-letter word. For example, in A?ENTV the ? could be an A, B, C, D or E. Here it represents a D, which can be combined with the other letters to spell ADVENT. The first letter is placed to get you started.

A C H T ? Y

C ☐ ☐ ☐ ☐ ☐

A F G ? R U

F ☐ ☐ ☐ ☐ ☐

A D F ? O R

A ☐ ☐ ☐ ☐ ☐

D F G I I ?

F ☐ ☐ ☐ ☐ ☐

A ? E G G U

G ☐ ☐ ☐ ☐ ☐

? E L M O U

M ☐ ☐ ☐ ☐ ☐

B D ? I I R

B ☐ ☐ ☐ ☐ ☐

B ? H M U U

H ☐ ☐ ☐ ☐ ☐

A D I R W ?

W ☐ ☐ ☐ ☐ ☐

C L M N O ?

C ☐ ☐ ☐ ☐ ☐

TOP BANANA

For each bunch below, rearrange the letters to form two intersecting words that fit into the corresponding grid.

BANANA CRUNCH

Each set of 10 tiles below contains two common five-letter words. The letters of the first five-letter word are adjacent, but not in order. Find them and rearrange them to spell a word. Cross out those letters and imagine that the five remaining letters are now consecutive. These remaining letters can now be rearranged to spell the second word.

Example: GTIAKLPOTH. AKLPO can be rearranged into **POLKA.** That leaves **GTITH,** which can be rearranged into **TIGHT.**

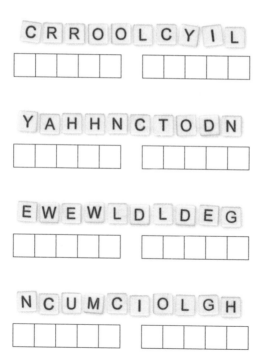

CRROOLCYIL

YAHHNCTODN

EWEWLDLDEG

NCUMCIOLGH

BANANA PUDDING

Each of the two-letter groups below may be extended both on the right and the left to form a six-letter word. Drawing from the tiles directly above each group, fill in the blanks to find the words as quickly as you can.

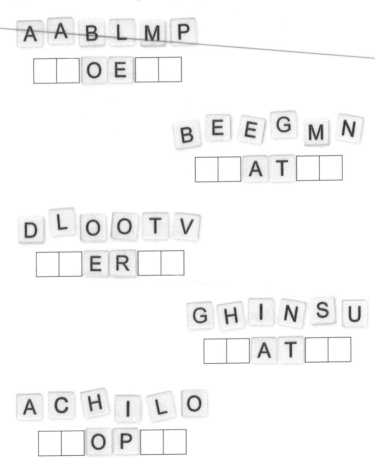

A A B L M P
☐ ☐ O E ☐ ☐

B E E G M N
☐ ☐ A T ☐ ☐

D L O O T V
☐ ☐ E R ☐ ☐

G H I N S U
☐ ☐ A T ☐ ☐

A C H I L O
☐ ☐ O P ☐ ☐

TOTALLY BANANAS

For each of the words below, replace one letter with the tile after the plus sign. Then rearrange the letters to form things that can be part of a song.

M O D E L S + Y

[ ] [ ] [ ] [ ] [ ] [ ]

S L I C E R + Y

[ ] [ ] [ ] [ ] [ ] [ ]

T A M E + B

[ ] [ ] [ ] [ ]

M O T E L + P

[ ] [ ] [ ] [ ] [ ]

S H R O U D + C

[ ] [ ] [ ] [ ] [ ] [ ]

S P R E E + V

[ ] [ ] [ ] [ ] [ ]

BANANA TREES

Use the 15 tiles in this bunch to create words that fit into the grids below. To get you started, a few tiles from the bunch have been placed in the grid. The BANANA BITES provide hints to help you solve each grid. Reuse the 15 tiles in the bunch for each grid.

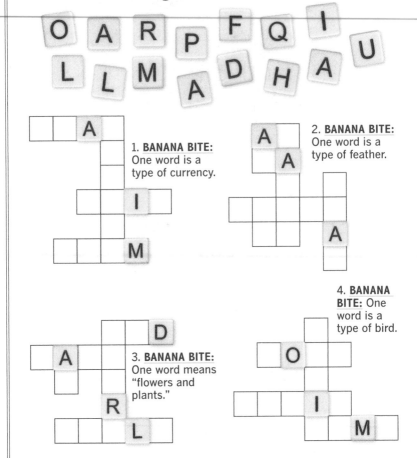

1. BANANA BITE: One word is a type of currency.

2. BANANA BITE: One word is a type of feather.

3. BANANA BITE: One word means "flowers and plants."

4. BANANA BITE: One word is a type of bird.

BUNCH OF BANANAS

For each word or phrase below, rearrange the letters to spell two new words that represent a pair of people who work together. For example, JULY RAGWEED can be rearranged to spell JUDGE, LAWYER. The first letter of each word is placed to get you started.

A FREE WITCH
C _ _ _   W _ _ _ _ _

I HELP CAPTURE
T _ _ _ _ _ _   P _ _ _ _

TACT WORRIER
W _ _ _ _ _   A _ _ _ _

TRUE CONDORS
D _ _ _ _   N _ _ _ _

A HOT TOUR RIDE
A _ _ _ _ _   E _ _ _ _ _

CARB TO BRAIN
R _ _ _ _   C _ _ _ _ _

37

BANANA BITES

Rearrange the letters of each word below and place them in the blanks so that, together with the two letters that have already been placed, they form a new word.

S O R E

P _ _ _ N

E L S E

A _ _ _ P

C O A L

L _ _ _ E

R A C E

S _ _ _ H

BANANA FILLING

Add a U to each of the words below and then rearrange the letters in each word to form a new six-letter word.

A D O R N

P A T I O

T R A I L

M I M E D

Using three of the tiles from the bunch on the left, fill in the blanks on the right to make a six-letter word that connects the grid.

A

D

C

I R

P S

U N I T

G U N

S T O R E

39

BANANA SHAKES

Each of the following six-letter sets can be rearranged to spell out a common word that either starts with `A B`, `D E`, or `I N` or ends with `O N`, `L Y`, or `E R`. Find all the words as quickly as you can.

A A B C S U

A C N N O Y

B I L S U Y

A B D E E T

A C E H R R

C E I I N T

C D D E E O

E F I N S U

C L M O P Y

B E H O R T

A D G N O R

A B C D T U

BANANA PEELS

There is <u>one letter</u> that when added to all of the four-letter words below can be used to form new five-letter words. Find the letter that works for all four words, add it to each word, and then rearrange each set of letters to form a new word. For example, B can be added to LOSS, ONLY, AUTO and IRON to form SLOBS, NOBLY, ABOUT and ROBIN.

COMMON
LETTER

[ ]

O R A L

[ ][ ][ ][ ][ ]

S E A T

[ ][ ][ ][ ][ ]

C A P S

[ ][ ][ ][ ][ ]

T I F F

[ ][ ][ ][ ][ ]

BANANARAMA

Each of the words below can be turned into another word on the list by changing one letter and then rearranging them all to form a new word. For example, REGIMENT can be turned into STEERING by changing the M to an S, so they would be a pair. How quickly can you find all the pairs?

Pairs

1. ALMOST   __ __

2. GOALIE   __ __

3. USAGES   __ __

4. WISDOM   __ __

5. COINED   __ __

6. OPTIMA

7. EPILOG

8. DOCILE

9. MIAOWS

10. SUBSEA

11. BITMAP

12. TOTALS

42

BANANA CHIPS

Each set of letters below is arranged alphabetically, and the
? is in the correct alphabetical position. Figure out what
letter the ? represents and rearrange the letters to spell
a six-letter word. For example, in A?ENTV the ? could be
an A, B, C, D or E. Here it represents a D, which can be
combined with the other letters to spell ADVENT. The first
letter is placed to get you started.

A E F G O ?

F ⬜⬜⬜⬜⬜

B ? E N O Y

B ⬜⬜⬜⬜⬜

B ? I L P U

P ⬜⬜⬜⬜⬜

D L L O O ?

D ⬜⬜⬜⬜⬜

E E E R R ?

R ⬜⬜⬜⬜⬜

D ? O O R X

O ⬜⬜⬜⬜⬜

D E O T ? X

T ⬜⬜⬜⬜⬜

D E N ? U U

U ⬜⬜⬜⬜⬜

? H I M S S

S ⬜⬜⬜⬜⬜

C E E F ? O

C ⬜⬜⬜⬜⬜

43

For each bunch below, rearrange the letters to form two intersecting words that fit into the corresponding grid.

BANANA CRUNCH

Each set of 10 tiles below contains two common five-letter words. The letters of the first five-letter word are adjacent, but not in order. Find them and rearrange them to spell a word. Cross out those letters and imagine that the five remaining letters are now consecutive. These remaining letters can now be rearranged to spell the second word.

Example: GTIAKLPOTH. AKLPO can be rearranged into POLKA. That leaves GTITH, which can be rearranged into TIGHT.

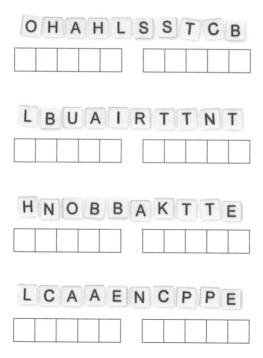

OHAHLSSTCB

LBUAIRTTNT

HNOBBAKTTE

LCAAENCPPE

BANANA PUDDING

Each of the two-letter groups below may be extended both on the right and the left to form a six-letter word. Drawing from the tiles directly above each group, fill in the blanks to find the words as quickly as you can.

```
A I P P R T
[ ][ ] O M [ ][ ]
```

```
E M N O R W
[ ][ ] O D [ ][ ]
```

```
C E E M O T
[ ][ ] U P [ ][ ]
```

```
C L O P R Y
[ ][ ] E N [ ][ ]
```

```
C E E L N R
[ ][ ] A M [ ][ ]
```

46

TOTALLY BANANAS

For each of the words below, replace one letter with the tile after the plus sign. Then rearrange the letters to form a popular card game.

PRONE + K

CHAINS + O

REHASH + T

INBRED + G

MURKY + M

LAPSES + D

BANANA TREES

Use the 15 tiles in this bunch to create words that fit into the grids below. To get you started, a few tiles from the bunch have been placed in the grid. The **BANANA BITES** provide hints to help you solve each grid. Reuse the 15 tiles in the bunch for each grid.

1. BANANA BITE: One word is something you can travel on.

2. BANANA BITE: One word means "leave out."

3. BANANA BITE: One word is a type of farm animal.

4. BANANA BITE: One word is a type of weapon.

48

BUNCH OF BANANAS

For each word or phrase below, rearrange the letters to spell two new words that are homonyms. For example, AGE WITH WIT can be rearranged to spell WAIT, WEIGHT. The first letter of each word is placed to get you started.

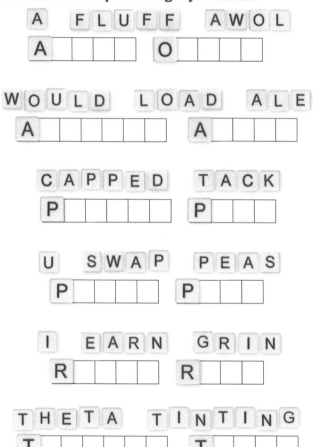

A FLUFF AWOL

A ☐ ☐ ☐ ☐   O ☐ ☐ ☐ ☐

WOULD LOAD ALE

A ☐ ☐ ☐ ☐ ☐ ☐   A ☐ ☐ ☐ ☐

CAPPED TACK

P ☐ ☐ ☐ ☐ ☐ ☐   P ☐ ☐ ☐

U SWAP PEAS

P ☐ ☐ ☐ ☐ ☐   P ☐ ☐ ☐

I EARN GRIN

R ☐ ☐ ☐ ☐   R ☐ ☐ ☐

THETA TINTING

T ☐ ☐ ☐ ☐ ☐   T ☐ ☐ ☐ ☐

Rearrange the letters of each word below and place them in the blanks so that, together with the two letters that have already been placed, they form a new word.

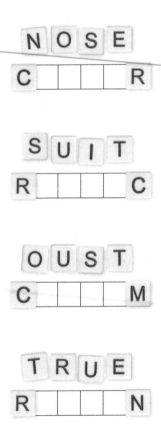

NOSE
C _ _ _ R

SUIT
R _ _ _ C

OUST
C _ _ _ M

TRUE
R _ _ _ N

BANANA FILLING

Add a `T` **to each of the words below and then rearrange the letters in each word to form a new six-letter word.**

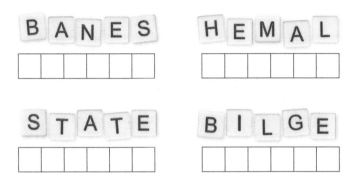

B A N E S

H E M A L

S T A T E

B I L G E

Using three of the tiles from the bunch on the left, fill in the blanks on the right to make a six-letter word that connects the grid.

BANANA SHAKES

Each of the following six-letter sets can be rearranged to spell out a common word that either starts with A M, B I, or C O or ends with E E, N T, or R T. Find all the words as quickly as you can.

B G G I I W

A C L L O R

A A L M O R

B E E G N U

D E E E G R

B C I I N O

A H R T T W

C E I L N T

A B C L O T

E I N R T V

A M N O T U

A F L N T U

BANANA PEELS

There is <u>one letter</u> that when added to all of the four-letter words below can be used to form new five-letter words. Find the letter that works for all four words, add it to each word, and then rearrange each set of letters to form a new word. For example, B can be added to LOSS, ONLY, AUTO and IRON to form SLOBS, NOBLY, ABOUT and ROBIN.

COMMON
LETTER

C A R S

D R A W

W E R E

H E R S

BANANARAMA

Each of the words below can be turned into another word on the list by changing one letter and then rearranging them all to form a new word. For example, REGIMENT can be turned into STEERING by changing the M to an S, so they would be a pair. How quickly can you find all the pairs?

Pairs

1. HEROIC   ___ ___

2. GLAMOR   ___ ___

3. HATTER   ___ ___

4. KEYPAD   ___ ___

5. RUGOLA   ___ ___

6. OILCUP

7. CHROME

8. DREDGE

9. THWART

10. PUBLIC

11. GEARED

12. YAUPED

54

BANANA CHIPS

Each set of letters below is arranged alphabetically, and the
? is in the correct alphabetical position. Figure out what
letter the ? represents and rearrange the letters to spell
a six-letter word. For example, in A?ENTV the ? could be
an A, B, C, D or E. Here it represents a D, which can be
combined with the other letters to spell ADVENT. The first
letter is placed to get you started.

? P P S U U

P ☐ ☐ ☐ ☐ ☐

A H I N ? V

V ☐ ☐ ☐ ☐ ☐

E E J ? S Y

J ☐ ☐ ☐ ☐ ☐

A ? L O P W

W ☐ ☐ ☐ ☐ ☐

A D F R ? Y

D ☐ ☐ ☐ ☐ ☐

A E N P ? U

P ☐ ☐ ☐ ☐ ☐

? E P R T W

P ☐ ☐ ☐ ☐ ☐

A A A ? M P

P ☐ ☐ ☐ ☐ ☐

A F ? O P Y

P ☐ ☐ ☐ ☐ ☐

A M ? T T U

M ☐ ☐ ☐ ☐ ☐

For each bunch below, rearrange the letters to form two intersecting words that fit into the corresponding grid.

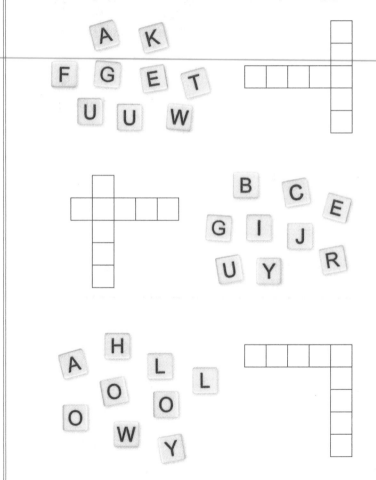

BANANA CRUNCH

Each set of 10 tiles below contains two common five-letter words. The letters of the first five-letter word are adjacent, but not in order. Find them and rearrange them to spell a word. Cross out those letters and imagine that the five remaining letters are now consecutive. These remaining letters can now be rearranged to spell the second word.

Example: GTIAKLPOTH. AKLPO can be rearranged into POLKA. That leaves GTITH, which can be rearranged into TIGHT.

T I N L L E A G F A

E E G V A H S S T R

U K Y G I O R R J N

T O R R F U D P E I

BANANA PUDDING

Each of the two-letter groups below may be extended both on the right and the left to form a six-letter word. Drawing from the tiles directly above each group, fill in the blanks to find the words as quickly as you can.

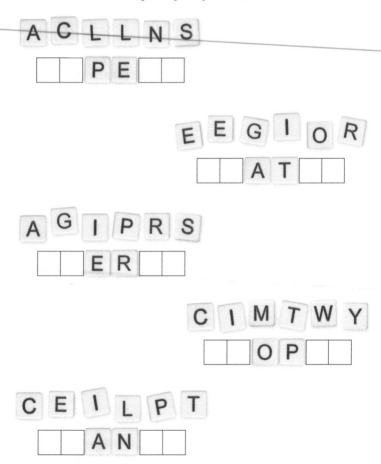

A C L L N S

☐ ☐ P E ☐ ☐

E E G I O R

☐ ☐ A T ☐ ☐

A G I P R S

☐ ☐ E R ☐ ☐

C I M T W Y

☐ ☐ O P ☐ ☐

C E I L P T

☐ ☐ A N ☐ ☐

TOTALLY BANANAS

For each of the words below, replace one letter with the tile after the plus sign. Then rearrange the letters to form an adjective that describes something visual.

A H O Y + Z

⬜⬜⬜⬜

A D O R N + U

⬜⬜⬜⬜⬜

R A N K + D

⬜⬜⬜⬜

B I R T H S + G

⬜⬜⬜⬜⬜⬜

C O R N E A + G

⬜⬜⬜⬜⬜⬜

P I T C H M A N + G

⬜⬜⬜⬜⬜⬜⬜⬜

BANANA TREES

Use the 15 tiles in this bunch to create words that fit into the grids below. To get you started, a few tiles from the bunch have been placed in the grid. The BANANA BITES provide hints to help you solve each grid. Reuse the 15 tiles in the bunch for each grid.

1. BANANA BITE: One word means "make beer."

2. BANANA BITE: One word is a type of fruit.

3. BANANA BITE: One word means "gone for awhile."

4. BANANA BITE: One word means "posh."

BUNCH OF BANANAS

For each word or phrase below, rearrange the letters to spell two new words that are opposites in meaning. For example, **WEAR CAPE** can be rearranged to spell **WAR, PEACE**. The first letter of each word is placed to get you started.

A PEAK   WEASEL

A ☐☐☐☐   A☐☐☐☐

THEFT   GIRL

R☐☐☐☐   L☐☐☐

STRANGE   WOK

S☐☐☐☐☐☐   W☐☐☐

NO MEANY

O☐☐   M☐☐☐

NIX TEETER

E☐☐☐☐   E☐☐☐

GLIB TITLE

B☐☐   L☐☐☐☐☐

Rearrange the letters of each word below and place them in the blanks so that, together with the two letters that have already been placed, they form a new word.

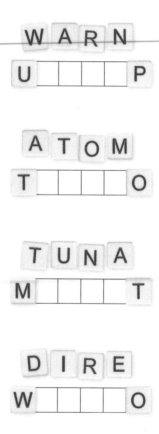

WARN

U _ _ _ P

ATOM

T _ _ _ O

TUNA

M _ _ _ T

DIRE

W _ _ _ O

BANANA FILLING

Add a W to each of the words below and then rearrange the letters in each word to form a new six-letter word.

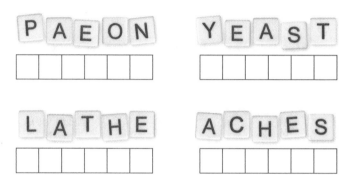

P A E O N

Y E A S T

L A T H E

A C H E S

Using three of the tiles from the bunch on the left, fill in the blanks on the right to make a six-letter word that connects the grid.

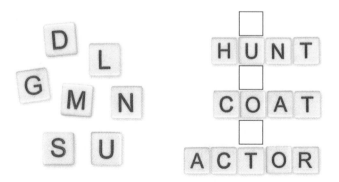

BANANA SHAKES

Each of the following six-letter sets can be rearranged to spell out a common word that either starts with S C, C O, or C R **or** ends with A N, E N, or I N. Find all the words as quickly as you can.

A C E M R Y

☐☐☐☐☐☐

C C N O O O

☐☐☐☐☐☐

A E E N N T

☐☐☐☐☐☐

F F I M N U

☐☐☐☐☐☐

C I P R S T

☐☐☐☐☐☐

C E I L L O

☐☐☐☐☐☐

A A D M M N

☐☐☐☐☐☐

C C E I N S

☐☐☐☐☐☐

A A I N T T

☐☐☐☐☐☐

C I I R S S

☐☐☐☐☐☐

A D E E M N

☐☐☐☐☐☐

A C E M N U

☐☐☐☐☐☐

64

BANANA PEELS

There is <u>one letter</u> that when added to all of the four-letter words below can be used to form new five-letter words. Find the letter that works for all four words, add it to each word, and then rearrange each set of letters to form a new word. For example, B can be added to LOSS, ONLY, AUTO and IRON to form SLOBS, NOBLY, ABOUT and ROBIN.

COMMON
LETTER

D U C T

C I T E

E D G E

B U Y S

BANANARAMA

Each of the words below can be turned into another word on the list by changing one letter and then rearranging them all to form a new word. For example, REGIMENT can be turned into STEERING by changing the M to an S, so they would be a pair. How quickly can you find all the pairs?

		Pairs
1.	E S C A P E	—— ——
2.	F A M I S H	—— ——
3.	P A L A T E	—— ——
4.	F I E R C E	—— ——
5.	I M B U E D	—— ——
6.	A L U M N I	
7.	S P E C I E	
8.	M U L I N G	
9.	B E D U I N	
10.	R E C I P E	
11.	M I S H A P	
12.	A C E T A L	

Each set of letters below is arranged alphabetically, and the ? is in the correct alphabetical position. Figure out what letter the ? represents and rearrange the letters to spell a six-letter word. For example, in A?ENTV the ? could be an A, B, C, D or E. Here it represents a D, which can be combined with the other letters to spell ADVENT. The first letter is placed to get you started.

E E M P T ?

E ⬚ ⬚ ⬚ ⬚ ⬚

E E H L M ?

H ⬚ ⬚ ⬚ ⬚ ⬚

E E ? N P W

N ⬚ ⬚ ⬚ ⬚ ⬚

E E ? L U Y

E ⬚ ⬚ ⬚ ⬚ ⬚

B C E N O ?

B ⬚ ⬚ ⬚ ⬚ ⬚

B ? E E O Y

O ⬚ ⬚ ⬚ ⬚ ⬚

? G N O X Y

O ⬚ ⬚ ⬚ ⬚ ⬚

C C I ? S U

C ⬚ ⬚ ⬚ ⬚ ⬚

E E L L P ?

P ⬚ ⬚ ⬚ ⬚ ⬚

E ? H N P Y

H ⬚ ⬚ ⬚ ⬚ ⬚

TOP BANANA

For each bunch below, rearrange the letters to form two intersecting words that fit into the corresponding grid.

BANANA CRUNCH

Each set of 10 tiles below contains two common five-letter words. The letters of the first five-letter word are adjacent, but not in order. Find them and rearrange them to spell a word. Cross out those letters and imagine that the five remaining letters are now consecutive. These remaining letters can now be rearranged to spell the second word.

Example: GTIAKLPOTH. AKLPO can be rearranged into POLKA. That leaves GTITH, which can be rearranged into TIGHT.

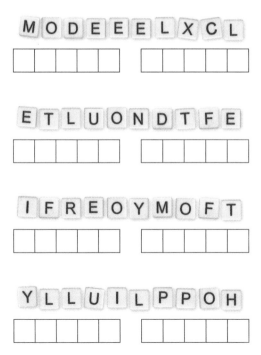

M O D E E E L X C L

E T L U O N D T F E

I F R E O Y M O F T

Y L L U I L P P O H

BANANA PUDDING

Each of the two-letter groups below may be extended both on the right and the left to form a six-letter word. Drawing from the tiles directly above each group, fill in the blanks to find the words as quickly as you can.

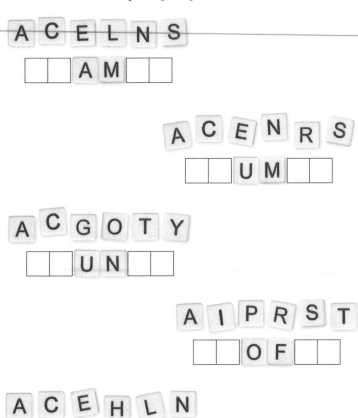

A C E L N S

☐ ☐ A M ☐ ☐

A C E N R S

☐ ☐ U M ☐ ☐

A C G O T Y

☐ ☐ U N ☐ ☐

A I P R S T

☐ ☐ O F ☐ ☐

A C E H L N

☐ ☐ O S ☐ ☐

TOTALLY BANANAS

**For each of the words below, replace one letter with the
tile after the plus sign. Then rearrange the letters to form
a common household tool.**

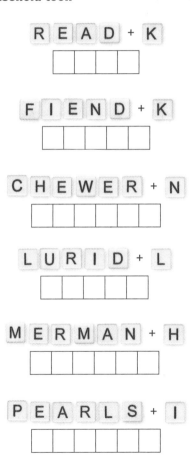

R E A D + K

F I E N D + K

C H E W E R + N

L U R I D + L

M E R M A N + H

P E A R L S + I

BANANA TREES

Use the 15 tiles in this bunch to create words that fit into the grids below. To get you started, a few tiles from the bunch have been placed in the grid. The BANANA BITES provide hints to help you solve each grid. Reuse the 15 tiles in the bunch for each grid.

1. BANANA BITE:
One word is a type of footwear.

2. BANANA BITE:
One word means "foreigners."

3. BANANA BITE:
One word means "speech."

4. BANANA BITE:
One word means "acquire."

BUNCH OF BANANAS

For each word or phrase below, rearrange the letters to spell two things that can be sharp. For example, SENTINEL COP can be rearranged to spell NOTES, PENCIL. The first letter of each word is placed to get you started.

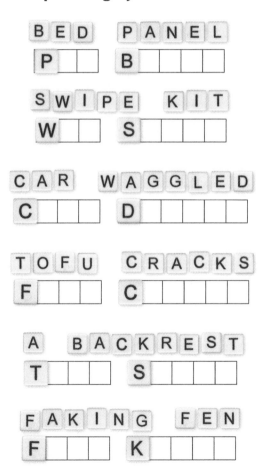

BED   PANEL

P ⬜ ⬜   B ⬜ ⬜ ⬜ ⬜

SWIPE   KIT

W ⬜ ⬜   S ⬜ ⬜ ⬜

CAR   WAGGLED

C ⬜ ⬜ ⬜   D ⬜ ⬜ ⬜ ⬜ ⬜

TOFU   CRACKS

F ⬜ ⬜ ⬜   C ⬜ ⬜ ⬜ ⬜ ⬜

A   BACKREST

T ⬜ ⬜ ⬜   S ⬜ ⬜ ⬜ ⬜

FAKING   FEN

F ⬜ ⬜ ⬜   K ⬜ ⬜ ⬜ ⬜

BANANA BITES

Rearrange the letters of each word below and place them in the blanks so that, together with the two letters that have already been placed, they form a new word.

CORN

B _ _ _ O

MARE

D _ _ _ Y

RIME

H _ _ _ T

ROAR

C _ _ _ T

BANANA FILLING

Add an [I] to each of the words below and then rearrange the letters in each word to form a new six-letter word.

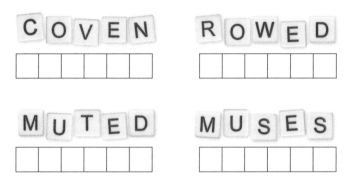

C O V E N

R O W E D

M U T E D

M U S E S

Using three of the tiles from the bunch on the left, fill in the blanks on the right to make a six-letter word that connects the grid.

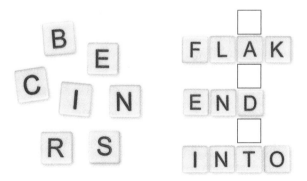

B
E
C
I N
R S

F L A K
E N D
I N T O

BANANA SHAKES

Each of the following six-letter sets can be rearranged to spell out a common word that either starts with `F R`**,** `I N`**, or** `P L` **or ends with** `C T`**,** `N D`**, or** `R D`**. Find all the words as quickly as you can.**

A F G L R U

C D D E T U

A E H I L N

A D P R U W

D F G I I R

D I N N U W

A D N O R W

D I N O O R

D E E G L P

C D I I N T

D G N O R U

G H L O P U

BANANA PEELS

There is <u>one letter</u> that when added to all of the four-letter words below can be used to form new five-letter words. Find the letter that works for all four words, add it to each word, and then rearrange each set of letters to form a new word. For example, **B** can be added to **LOSS**, **ONLY**, **AUTO** and **IRON** to form **SLOBS**, **NOBLY**, **ABOUT** and **ROBIN**.

COMMON
LETTER

N E A R

T A I L

L U A U

Y E A H

BANANARAMA

Each of the words below can be turned into another word on the list by changing one letter and then rearranging them all to form a new word. For example, REGIMENT can be turned into STEERING by changing the M to an S, so they would be a pair. How quickly can you find all the pairs?

Pairs

1. G A G M A N

—— ——

2. A N C H O R

—— ——

3. S L O U G H

—— ——

4. N O R D I C

—— ——

5. T A M A L E

—— ——

6. E N C O D E

7. C A R B O N

8. A F L A M E

9. M A G I A N

10. G A L O S H

11. D O C E N T

12. O R D A I N

78

BANANA CHIPS

Each set of letters below is arranged alphabetically, and the ? is in the correct alphabetical position. Figure out what letter the ? represents and rearrange the letters to spell a six-letter word. For example, in A?ENTV the ? could be an A, B, C, D or E. Here it represents a D, which can be combined with the other letters to spell ADVENT. The first letter is placed to get you started.

E G I ? P P

P ☐ ☐ ☐ ☐ ☐

C I I ? S S

C ☐ ☐ ☐ ☐ ☐

E I ? S U W

U ☐ ☐ ☐ ☐ ☐

E H I L ? U

H ☐ ☐ ☐ ☐ ☐

E G H ? O U

E ☐ ☐ ☐ ☐ ☐

E ? I N T Z

Z ☐ ☐ ☐ ☐ ☐

E G H I O ?

H ☐ ☐ ☐ ☐ ☐

B D I I ? T

T ☐ ☐ ☐ ☐ ☐

E F O R ? V

F ☐ ☐ ☐ ☐ ☐

E ? P R Y Z

Z ☐ ☐ ☐ ☐ ☐

79

TOP BANANA

For each bunch below, rearrange the letters to form two intersecting words that fit into the corresponding grid.

BANANA CRUNCH

Each set of 10 tiles below contains two common five-letter words. The letters of the first five-letter word are adjacent, but not in order. Find them and rearrange them to spell a word. Cross out those letters and imagine that the five remaining letters are now consecutive. These remaining letters can now be rearranged to spell the second word.

Example: GTIAKLPOTH. AKLPO can be rearranged into POLKA. That leaves GTITH, which can be rearranged into TIGHT.

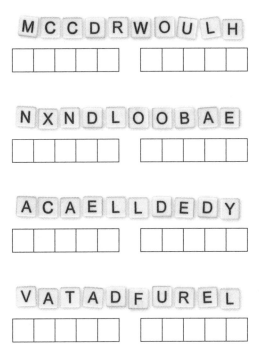

MCCDRWOULH

NXNDLOOBAE

ACAELLDEDY

VATADFUREL

BANANA PUDDING

Each of the two-letter groups below may be extended both on the right and the left to form a six-letter word. Drawing from the tiles directly above each group, fill in the blanks to find the words as quickly as you can.

B E N N O U

| | | I | S | | |

B E G M R S

| | | O | I | | |

D E E M R T

| | | N | U | | |

B E N O S T

| | | E | R | | |

E G I M R T

| | | N | O | | |

TOTALLY BANANAS

For each of the words below, replace one letter with the tile after the plus sign. Then rearrange the letters to form a type of shape.

QUEASY + R

☐☐☐☐☐☐

REPOSE + H

☐☐☐☐☐☐

RECOIL + C

☐☐☐☐☐☐

CRATE + H

☐☐☐☐☐

NOMADIC + D

☐☐☐☐☐☐☐

LIPLESS + E

☐☐☐☐☐☐☐

83

BANANA TREES

Use the 15 tiles in this bunch to create words that fit into the grids below. To get you started, a few tiles from the bunch have been placed in the grid. The BANANA BITES provide hints to help you solve each grid. Reuse the 15 tiles in the bunch for each grid.

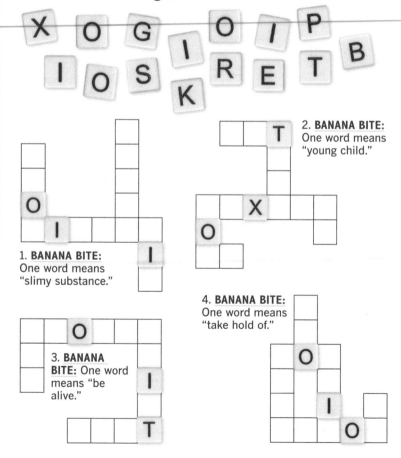

1. BANANA BITE:
One word means "slimy substance."

2. BANANA BITE:
One word means "young child."

3. BANANA BITE: One word means "be alive."

4. BANANA BITE:
One word means "take hold of."

BUNCH OF BANANAS

For each word or phrase below, rearrange the letters to spell two new words that can both be combined with the suffix –BALL to form a compound word. For example, SOD DOWN can be rearranged to spell ODD (ball) and SNOW (ball). The first letter of each word is placed to get you started.

CRAB → B ☐ ☐ ☐   NOSE → C ☐ ☐ ☐

BATON → F ☐ ☐ ☐   FOE → B ☐ ☐

TIRE → F ☐ ☐ ☐   FAME → M ☐ ☐ ☐

SOOT → G ☐ ☐ ☐   GAFF → F ☐ ☐ ☐

I TAR → S ☐ ☐ ☐   SHIP → H ☐ ☐ ☐

BEAN → B ☐ ☐ ☐ ☐   CHIP → P ☐ ☐

Rearrange the letters of each word below and place them in the blanks so that, together with the two letters that have already been placed, they form a new word.

B A R E

N _ _ _ Y

W A D I

M _ _ _ Y

T I N E

Z _ _ _ H

G O R E

F _ _ _ T

Add an O to each of the words below and then rearrange the letters in each word to form a new six-letter word.

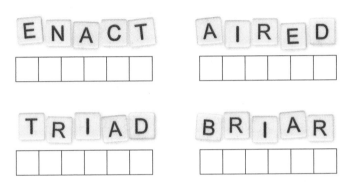

E N A C T

⬜⬜⬜⬜⬜⬜

A I R E D

⬜⬜⬜⬜⬜⬜

T R I A D

⬜⬜⬜⬜⬜⬜

B R I A R

⬜⬜⬜⬜⬜⬜

Using three of the tiles from the bunch on the left, fill in the blanks on the right to make a six-letter word that connects the grid.

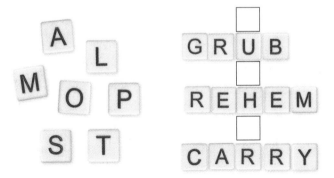

A
M L
O P
S T

G R U B
R E H E M
C A R R Y

BANANA SHAKES

Each of the following six-letter sets can be rearranged to spell out a common word that either starts with ME, PE, or DE or ends with CH, CK, or IC. Find all the words as quickly as you can.

C E H I N T

C F H I L N

D E L M O Y

A C K N P U

E I L P S V

C F I L O R

A A C K T T

C D E E I T

C G H O R U

C E I L N P

E I M M O R

A D E E F L

BANANA PEELS

There is <u>one letter</u> that when added to all of the four-letter words below can be used to form new five-letter words. Find the letter that works for all four words, add it to each word, and then rearrange each set of letters to form a new word. For example, B can be added to LOSS, ONLY, AUTO and IRON to form SLOBS, NOBLY, ABOUT and ROBIN.

COMMON
LETTER

[ ]

Y A W L

[ ][ ][ ][ ][ ]

D E E M

[ ][ ][ ][ ][ ]

G O O N

[ ][ ][ ][ ][ ]

I O N S

[ ][ ][ ][ ][ ]

BANANARAMA

Each of the words below can be turned into another word on the list by changing one letter and then rearranging them all to form a new word. For example, REGIMENT can be turned into STEERING by changing the M to an S, so they would be a pair. How quickly can you find all the pairs?

Pairs

1. U N C U T E   —— ——
2. T A R S U S   —— ——
3. O U T B E G   —— ——
4. U P D A R T   —— ——
5. C A T G U T   —— ——
6. G U I T A R
7. B U D G E T
8. W U R S T S
9. P U T R I D
10. O U T R I G
11. O U T A C T
12. T U N E U P

BANANA CHIPS

Each set of letters below is arranged alphabetically, and the ? **is in the correct alphabetical position. Figure out what letter the** ? **represents and rearrange the letters to spell a six-letter word. For example, in A?ENTV the** ? **could be an A, B, C, D or E. Here it represents a D, which can be combined with the other letters to spell ADVENT. The first letter is placed to get you started.**

E E K ? N N
K ☐ ☐ ☐ ☐ ☐

C E F I N ?
I ☐ ☐ ☐ ☐ ☐

E E M N ? Z
E ☐ ☐ ☐ ☐ ☐

D E O O ? V
O ☐ ☐ ☐ ☐ ☐

A E E N U ?
A ☐ ☐ ☐ ☐ ☐

A E L R W ?
L ☐ ☐ ☐ ☐ ☐

D ? I P S U
U ☐ ☐ ☐ ☐ ☐

E F ? N N U
F ☐ ☐ ☐ ☐ ☐

E I ? S T Y
S ☐ ☐ ☐ ☐ ☐

A ? E K P T
P ☐ ☐ ☐ ☐ ☐

TOP BANANA

For each bunch below, rearrange the letters to form two intersecting words that fit into the corresponding grid.

BANANA CRUNCH

Each set of 10 tiles below contains two common five-letter words. The letters of the first five-letter word are adjacent, but not in order. Find them and rearrange them to spell a word. Cross out those letters and imagine that the five remaining letters are now consecutive. These remaining letters can now be rearranged to spell the second word.

Example: GTIAKLPOTH. AKLPO can be rearranged into POLKA. That leaves GTITH, which can be rearranged into TIGHT.

L N B I O J T N A A

G G W N I R I L I V

E H T A K E W U S O

A O K I A H K O Z K

BANANA PUDDING

Each of the two-letter groups below may be extended both on the right and the left to form a six-letter word. Drawing from the tiles directly above each group, fill in the blanks to find the words as quickly as you can.

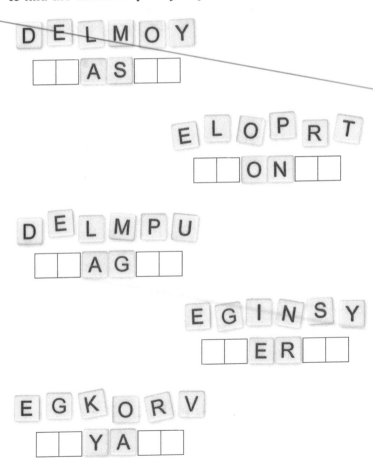

D E L M O Y

☐ ☐ A S ☐ ☐

E L O P R T

☐ ☐ O N ☐ ☐

D E L M P U

☐ ☐ A G ☐ ☐

E G I N S Y

☐ ☐ E R ☐ ☐

E G K O R V

☐ ☐ Y A ☐ ☐

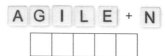

TOTALLY BANANAS

For each of the words below, replace one letter with the tile after the plus sign. Then rearrange the letters to form a word related to mathematics.

A G I L E + N

☐ ☐ ☐ ☐ ☐

S H A R P + G

☐ ☐ ☐ ☐ ☐

I M P E L + R

☐ ☐ ☐ ☐ ☐

T I M I D + G

☐ ☐ ☐ ☐ ☐

G U A R D S + I

☐ ☐ ☐ ☐ ☐ ☐

C A V O R T + F

☐ ☐ ☐ ☐ ☐ ☐

BANANA TREES

Use the 15 tiles in this bunch to create words that fit into the grids below. To get you started, a few tiles from the bunch have been placed in the grid. The BANANA BITES provide hints to help you solve each grid. Reuse the 15 tiles in the bunch for each grid.

1. BANANA BITE: One word is a number.

2. BANANA BITE: One word is a type of wig.

3. BANANA BITE: One word is a hair color.

4. BANANA BITE: One word means "excellent."

BUNCH OF BANANAS

For each word or phrase below, rearrange the letters to spell two things that can be white. For example, FOAMY SOLS can be rearranged to spell FLOSS MAYO. The first letter of each word is placed to get you started.

LIMERICK
M _ _ _ _   R _ _ _ _

I SO VAPORY
I _ _ _ _ _   S _ _ _

A RED BLAST
S _ _ _   B _ _ _ _

BOUNTIES
N _ _ _ _ _   T _ _

I OWN LOGOS
S _ _ _   I _ _ _ _

NIGHT LADS
L _ _ _ _   S _ _ _

Rearrange the letters of each word below and place them in the blanks so that, together with the two letters that have already been placed, they form a new word.

M U T E

N _ _ _ G

P E S O

G _ _ _ _ L

I C E S

B _ _ _ T

L O A M

S _ _ _ N

BANANA FILLING

Add an L to each of the words below and then rearrange the letters in each word to form a new six-letter word.

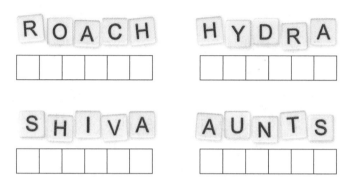

R O A C H

H Y D R A

S H I V A

A U N T S

Using three of the tiles from the bunch on the left, fill in the blanks on the right to make a six-letter word that connects the grid.

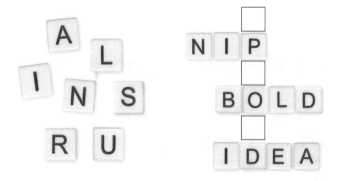

A
L
I
N S
R U

N I P
BOLD
IDEA

BANANA SHAKES

Each of the following six-letter sets can be rearranged to spell out a common word that either starts with EM, TH, or WR or ends with AW, AT, or LT. Find all the words as quickly as you can.

C E H N R W	E L O R T V

A F N N O T	A H H R S T

A E N S T U	A E E S S W

E H O R T Y	A L O T U W

B E M O R Y	L M T T U U

E R S T W Y	E L M O P Y

BANANA PEELS

There is <u>one letter</u> that when added to all of the four-letter words below can be used to form new five-letter words. Find the letter that works for all four words, add it to each word, and then rearrange each set of letters to form a new word. For example, B can be added to LOSS, ONLY, AUTO and IRON to form SLOBS, NOBLY, ABOUT and ROBIN.

COMMON
LETTER

RAFT

MALT

WHIG

BOOS

Each of the words below can be turned into another word on the list by changing one letter and then rearranging them all to form a new word. For example, REGIMENT can be turned into STEERING by changing the M to an S, so they would be a pair. How quickly can you find all the pairs?

Pairs

1. F E U D A L
2. T O N G E D
3. U N C L A D
4. D E N O T E
5. N A U S E A
6. S P I L T H
7. C A N D L E
8. P A L I S H
9. D O G E A R
10. A I D F U L
11. U N S A F E
12. L O D G E R

_____ _____

_____ _____

_____ _____

_____ _____

_____ _____

BANANA CHIPS

Each set of letters below is arranged alphabetically, and the ? is in the correct alphabetical position. Figure out what letter the ? represents and rearrange the letters to spell a six-letter word. For example, in A?ENTV the ? could be an A, B, C, D or E. Here it represents a D, which can be combined with the other letters to spell ADVENT. The first letter is placed to get you started.

A F H ? O T

F ☐ ☐ ☐ ☐ ☐

A D G ? L Y

G ☐ ☐ ☐ ☐ ☐

A H I M O ?

M ☐ ☐ ☐ ☐ ☐

B H I O ? S

B ☐ ☐ ☐ ☐ ☐

D H L O S ?

S ☐ ☐ ☐ ☐ ☐

B E O ? T W

B ☐ ☐ ☐ ☐ ☐

C I ? P P U

P ☐ ☐ ☐ ☐ ☐

A D ? O P R

P ☐ ☐ ☐ ☐ ☐

? N O O T Y

T ☐ ☐ ☐ ☐ ☐

A F L O ? V

F ☐ ☐ ☐ ☐ ☐

TOP BANANA

For each bunch below, rearrange the letters to form two intersecting words that fit into the corresponding grid.

BANANA CRUNCH

Each set of 10 tiles below contains two common five-letter words. The letters of the first five-letter word are adjacent, but not in order. Find them and rearrange them to spell a word. Cross out those letters and imagine that the five remaining letters are now consecutive. These remaining letters can now be rearranged to spell the second word.

Example: GTIAKLPOTH. AKLPO can be rearranged into POLKA. That leaves GTITH, which can be rearranged into TIGHT.

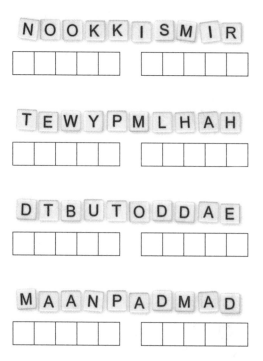

N O O K K I S M I R

T E W Y P M L H A H

D T B U T O D D A E

M A A N P A D M A D

BANANA PUDDING

Each of the two-letter groups below may be extended both on the right and the left to form a six-letter word. Drawing from the tiles directly above each group, fill in the blanks to find the words as quickly as you can.

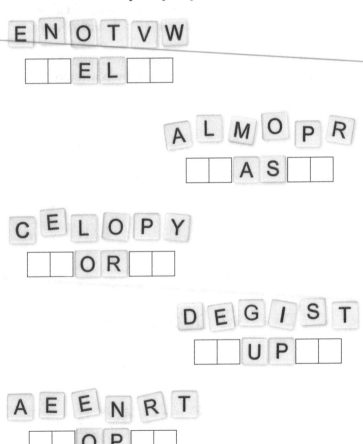

E N O T V W

☐ ☐ E L ☐ ☐

A L M O P R

☐ ☐ A S ☐ ☐

C E L O P Y

☐ ☐ O R ☐ ☐

D E G I S T

☐ ☐ U P ☐ ☐

A E E N R T

☐ ☐ O P ☐ ☐

TOTALLY BANANAS

For each of the words below, replace one letter with the tile
after the plus sign. Then rearrange the letters to form the
name of a popular board game.

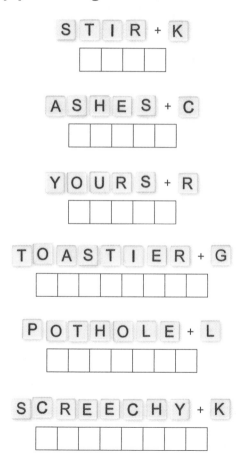

S T I R + K

☐ ☐ ☐ ☐

A S H E S + C

☐ ☐ ☐ ☐ ☐

Y O U R S + R

☐ ☐ ☐ ☐ ☐

T O A S T I E R + G

☐ ☐ ☐ ☐ ☐ ☐ ☐ ☐

P O T H O L E + L

☐ ☐ ☐ ☐ ☐ ☐ ☐

S C R E E C H Y + K

☐ ☐ ☐ ☐ ☐ ☐ ☐ ☐

BANANA TREES

Use the 15 tiles in this bunch to create words that fit into the grids below. To get you started, a few tiles from the bunch have been placed in the grid. The **BANANA BITES** provide hints to help you solve each grid. Reuse the 15 tiles in the bunch for each grid.

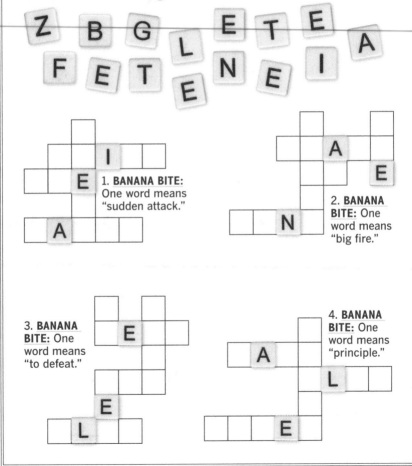

1. BANANA BITE: One word means "sudden attack."

2. BANANA BITE: One word means "big fire."

3. BANANA BITE: One word means "to defeat."

4. BANANA BITE: One word means "principle."

108

BUNCH OF BANANAS

For each word or phrase below, rearrange the letters to spell two new words that are synonyms. For example, WIZARD PEAR can be rearranged to spell AWARD, PRIZE. The first letter of each word is placed to get you started.

BILGE RAG
L▢▢▢▢▢   B▢▢

CRADLE REST
R▢▢   S▢▢▢▢▢▢

BELAUDS
B▢▢▢   S▢▢

WOMAN PASSER
A▢▢▢   W▢▢▢▢▢▢

NUTTY LOCAL
C▢▢▢▢▢   T▢▢▢▢

REVOLT CHEERS
C▢▢▢▢   S▢▢▢▢▢▢

BANANA BITES

Rearrange the letters of each word below and place them in the blanks so that, together with the two letters that have already been placed, they form a new word.

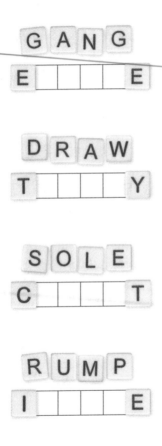

G A N G
E _ _ _ E

D R A W
T _ _ _ Y

S O L E
C _ _ _ T

R U M P
I _ _ _ E

BANANA FILLING

Add a **Y** to each of the words below and then rearrange the letters in each word to form a new six-letter word.

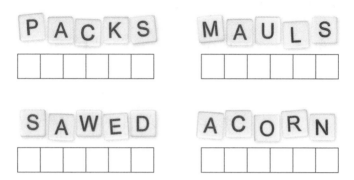

P A C K S

☐☐☐☐☐☐

M A U L S

☐☐☐☐☐☐

S A W E D

☐☐☐☐☐☐

A C O R N

☐☐☐☐☐☐

Using three of the tiles from the bunch on the left, fill in the blanks on the right to make a six-letter word that connects the grid.

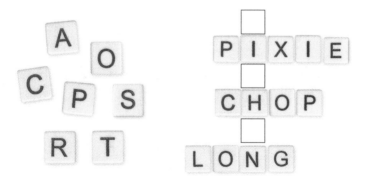

A
O
C
P   S
R   T

☐
P I X I E
☐
C H O P
☐
L O N G

BANANA SHAKES

Each of the following six-letter sets can be rearranged to spell out a common word that either starts with `AN`, `MA`, or `PR` or ends with `EN`, `IC`, or `ED`. Find all the words as quickly as you can.

A E L M N W

E O P P R R

B C I I O P

A H N O W Y

C D E E H O

A A D L M Y

C E I N P R

A E G L N R

B E K N O R

C I I N O R

A A C D M P

B D E I M U

BANANA PEELS

There is <u>one letter</u> that when added to all of the four-letter words below can be used to form new five-letter words. Find the letter that works for all four words, add it to each word, and then rearrange each set of letters to form a new word. For example, B can be added to LOSS, ONLY, AUTO and IRON to form SLOBS, NOBLY, ABOUT and ROBIN.

COMMON
LETTER

HAWK

HEFT

UNTO

MUSH

BANANARAMA

Each of the words below can be turned into another word on the list by changing one letter and then rearranging them all to form a new word. For example, REGIMENT can be turned into STEERING by changing the M to an S, so they would be a pair. How quickly can you find all the pairs?

		Pairs
1.	I L L U D E	___ ___
2.	R E R A C K	___ ___
3.	T E D I U M	___ ___
4.	R I P S A W	___ ___
5.	U N S E A T	___ ___
6.	O R A C L E	
7.	D I M O U T	
8.	S U N T A N	
9.	P S Y W A R	
10.	C U R A R E	
11.	A U D I L E	
12.	E C L A I R	

BANANA CHIPS

Each set of letters below is arranged alphabetically, and the ? is in the correct alphabetical position. Figure out what letter the ? represents and rearrange the letters to spell a six-letter word. For example, in A?ENTV the ? could be an A, B, C, D or E. Here it represents a D, which can be combined with the other letters to spell ADVENT. The first letter is placed to get you started.

A G L L ? O
G ☐ ☐ ☐ ☐ ☐

A ? D I O Z
Z ☐ ☐ ☐ ☐ ☐

A M O O T ?
T ☐ ☐ ☐ ☐ ☐

A C E F T ?
F ☐ ☐ ☐ ☐ ☐

A L ? S U W
W ☐ ☐ ☐ ☐ ☐

B D E H I ?
B ☐ ☐ ☐ ☐ ☐

? E L O T Z
Z ☐ ☐ ☐ ☐ ☐

A H M R ? W
W ☐ ☐ ☐ ☐ ☐

? E E H N V
H ☐ ☐ ☐ ☐ ☐

A I M R ? X
M ☐ ☐ ☐ ☐ ☐

TOP BANANA

For each bunch below, rearrange the letters to form two intersecting words that fit into the corresponding grid.

BANANA CRUNCH

Each set of 10 tiles below contains two common five-letter words. The letters of the first five-letter word are adjacent, but not in order. Find them and rearrange them to spell a word. Cross out those letters and imagine that the five remaining letters are now consecutive. These remaining letters can now be rearranged to spell the second word.

Example: GTIAKLPOTH. AKLPO can be rearranged into POLKA. That leaves GTITH, which can be rearranged into TIGHT.

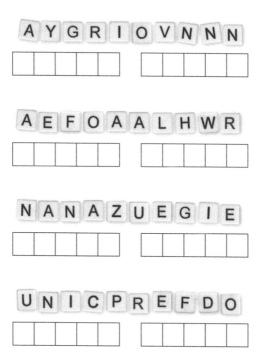

A Y G R I O V N N N

A E F O A A L H W R

N A N A Z U E G I E

U N I C P R E F D O

BANANA PUDDING

Each of the two-letter groups below may be extended both on the right and the left to form a six-letter word. Drawing from the tiles directly above each group, fill in the blanks to find the words as quickly as you can.

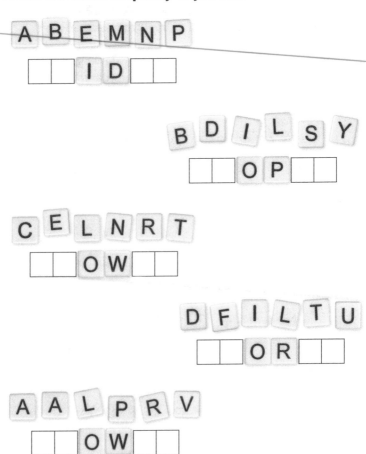

A B E M N P

☐ ☐ I D ☐ ☐

B D I L S Y

☐ ☐ O P ☐ ☐

C E L N R T

☐ ☐ O W ☐ ☐

D F I L T U

☐ ☐ O R ☐ ☐

A A L P R V

☐ ☐ O W ☐ ☐

TOTALLY BANANAS

For each of the words below, replace one letter with the tile after the plus sign. Then rearrange the letters to form an animal.

E R G O + F

☐ ☐ ☐ ☐

C O N F A B + L

☐ ☐ ☐ ☐ ☐ ☐

P T O O E Y + C

☐ ☐ ☐ ☐ ☐ ☐

L I P R E A D + O

☐ ☐ ☐ ☐ ☐ ☐ ☐

H O N E Y + A

☐ ☐ ☐ ☐ ☐

A D A P T + N

☐ ☐ ☐ ☐ ☐

BANANA TREES

Use the 15 tiles in this bunch to create words that fit into the grids below. To get you started, a few tiles from the bunch have been placed in the grid. The BANANA BITES provide hints to help you solve each grid. Reuse the 15 tiles in the bunch for each grid.

1. BANANA BITE:
One word means "dislike strongly."

2. BANANA BITE:
One word means "in a state of shock."

3. BANANA BITE:
One word means "a dangerous thing."

4. BANANA BITE:
One word is a type of hat.

BUNCH OF BANANAS

For each word or phrase below, rearrange the letters to spell two new words that are each types of curved or circular objects. For example, BIGGER FEES can be rearranged to spell EGG, FRISBEE. The first letter of each word is placed to get you started.

A   CAPER
A □ □   P □ □

COLT   CRIED
C □ □ □ □ □   D □ □

RUNT   SHEEP
N □ □   S □ □ □ □ □

YETI   ROBE
E □ □ □   O □ □ □ □

BUGLE   BLAB
B □ □ □   B □ □ □ □

PUNT   LANES
P □ □ □ □ □   S □ □

121

BANANA BITES

Rearrange the letters of each word below and place them in the blanks so that, together with the two letters that have already been placed, they form a new word.

R A I D

O _ _ _ N

B O R N

E _ _ _ E

W A R N

B _ _ _ Y

C O I L

P _ _ _ E

BANANA FILLING

Add a K to each of the words below and then rearrange the letters in each word to form a new six-letter word.

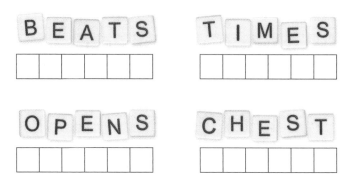

BEATS

TIMES

OPENS

CHEST

Using three of the tiles from the bunch on the left, fill in the blanks on the right to make a six-letter word that connects the grid.

BANANA SHAKES

Each of the following six-letter sets can be rearranged to spell out a common word that either starts with AD, DR, or TR or ends with AL, LE, or AN. Find all the words as quickly as you can.

A E H I L W

D D E E G R

A A E I L R

E E L O P P

A D E N T V

A H N O P R

H O P R T Y

A A M R T U

A D F I R T

A A L N N U

D O R S W Y

A B D E N P

There is <u>one letter</u> that when added to all of the four-letter words below can be used to form new five-letter words. Find the letter that works for all four words, add it to each word, and then rearrange each set of letters to form a new word. For example, B can be added to LOSS, ONLY, AUTO and IRON to form SLOBS, NOBLY, ABOUT and ROBIN.

COMMON
LETTER

D Y A D

T O A D

H I S S

L I M B

BANANARAMA

Each of the words below can be turned into another word on the list by changing one letter and then rearranging them all to form a new word. For example, REGIMENT can be turned into STEERING by changing the M to an S, so they would be a pair. How quickly can you find all the pairs?

Pairs

1. M Y O P I A ___ ___

2. U N R E A D ___ ___

3. M I D A I R ___ ___

4. F O I B L E ___ ___

5. P U E B L O ___ ___

6. H A R D E N

7. D I R E C T

8. B E L I E F

9. L I P O M A

10. T I D I E R

11. D O U B L E

12. R A D I U M

126

BANANA CHIPS

Each set of letters below is arranged alphabetically, and the ? is in the correct alphabetical position. Figure out what letter the ? represents and rearrange the letters to spell a six-letter word. For example, in A?ENTV the ? could be an A, B, C, D or E. Here it represents a D, which can be combined with the other letters to spell ADVENT. The first letter is placed to get you started.

? E I I L T
E _ _ _ _ _

E E F ? O T
T _ _ _ _ _

B ? N O U Y
B _ _ _ _ _

D I M O P ?
P _ _ _ _ _

B G L ? O O
O _ _ _ _ _

A ? H T T U
T _ _ _ _ _

A C I T V ?
C _ _ _ _ _

E ? M O U V
V _ _ _ _ _

B ? O T T U
B _ _ _ _ _

A A L M ? Y
L _ _ _ _ _

127

TOP BANANA

For each bunch below, rearrange the letters to form two intersecting words that fit into the corresponding grid.

128

BANANA CRUNCH

Each set of 10 tiles below contains two common five-letter words. The letters of the first five-letter word are adjacent, but not in order. Find them and rearrange them to spell a word. Cross out those letters and imagine that the five remaining letters are now consecutive. These remaining letters can now be rearranged to spell the second word.

Example: GTIAKLPOTH. AKLPO can be rearranged into POLKA. That leaves GTITH, which can be rearranged into TIGHT.

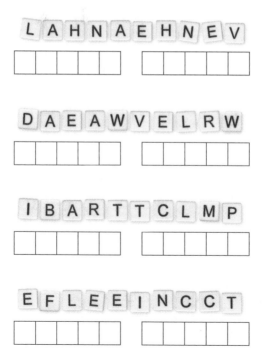

L A H N A E H N E V

D A E A W V E L R W

I B A R T T C L M P

E F L E E I N C C T

BANANA PUDDING

Each of the two-letter groups below may be extended both on the right and the left to form a six-letter word. Drawing from the tiles directly above each group, fill in the blanks to find the words as quickly as you can.

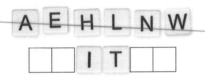

A E H L N W

☐ ☐ I T ☐ ☐

E E L N P R

☐ ☐ A B ☐ ☐

A C E N T U

☐ ☐ A N ☐ ☐

B C G N O O

☐ ☐ U P ☐ ☐

B D E N T U

☐ ☐ O Y ☐ ☐

TOTALLY BANANAS

For each of the words below, replace one letter with the tile after the plus sign. Then rearrange the letters to form one of the chemical elements.

C O M B I N E + R

☐ ☐ ☐ ☐ ☐ ☐ ☐

M A N G O + R

☐ ☐ ☐ ☐ ☐

C R U C I A L + M

☐ ☐ ☐ ☐ ☐ ☐ ☐

S O L I C I T + N

☐ ☐ ☐ ☐ ☐ ☐ ☐

G U M M I N E S S + A

☐ ☐ ☐ ☐ ☐ ☐ ☐ ☐ ☐

C H U M M I E R + O

☐ ☐ ☐ ☐ ☐ ☐ ☐ ☐

BANANA TREES

Use the 15 tiles in this bunch to create words that fit into the grids below. To get you started, a few tiles from the bunch have been placed in the grid. The BANANA BITES provide hints to help you solve each grid. Reuse the 15 tiles in the bunch for each grid.

M G E R E T G
I A N P E E V C

1. BANANA BITE: One word means "a strange person."

E

E

T

2. BANANA BITE: One word means "making."

N

E M

3. BANANA BITE: One word means "say hello."

M E

E

4. BANANA BITE: One word is a type of gathering.

T

E

G

BUNCH OF BANANAS

For each word or phrase below, rearrange the letters to spell two new words that describe emotional states. For example, **I DUST COURIER** can be rearranged to spell **CURIOUS, TIRED**. The first letter of each word is placed to get you started.

S U P E **F E A T S**
U ☐ ☐ ☐ ☐   S ☐ ☐ ☐ ☐

W R Y **D O U R** **A P E**
W ☐ ☐ ☐ ☐   P ☐ ☐ ☐ ☐ ☐

S C A L D E D **R A G**
G ☐ ☐ ☐   S ☐ ☐ ☐ ☐ ☐

S U E D E **C L O V E R**
S ☐ ☐ ☐ ☐ ☐   L ☐ ☐ ☐ ☐

G O R Y **E R A S E R**
E ☐ ☐ ☐ ☐   S ☐ ☐ ☐ ☐

L A D D E R **E X A M**
M ☐ ☐   R ☐ ☐ ☐ ☐ ☐ ☐

133

Rearrange the letters of each word below and place them in the blanks so that, together with the two letters that have already been placed, they form a new word.

M A R E

C _ _ _ A

M A U L

U _ _ _ T

R A I N

M _ _ _ A

V E I N

S _ _ _ L

BANANA FILLING

Add an A to each of the words below and then rearrange the letters in each word to form a new six-letter word.

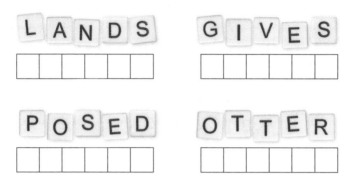

L A N D S

☐ ☐ ☐ ☐ ☐ ☐

G I V E S

☐ ☐ ☐ ☐ ☐ ☐

P O S E D

☐ ☐ ☐ ☐ ☐ ☐

O T T E R

☐ ☐ ☐ ☐ ☐ ☐

Using three of the tiles from the bunch on the left, fill in the blanks on the right to make a six-letter word that connects the grid.

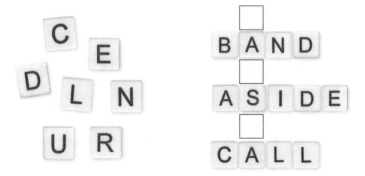

C
E
D
L N
U R

☐
B A N D
☐
A S I D E
☐
C A L L

BANANA SHAKES

Each of the following six-letter sets can be rearranged to spell out a common word that either starts with `A C`**,** `C H`**, or** `T H` **or ends with** `I A`**,** `N A`**, or** `T A`**. Find all the words as quickly as you can.**

A C C D I I

E H O R T Y

A A A B N N

C E E E H S

A A N O S T

H I R S T T

A I M O P Y

A A C L T U

A A A B C N

A E H I N R

A A E R R T

C D E H I M

BANANA PEELS

There is <u>one letter</u> that when added to all of the four-letter words below can be used to form new five-letter words. Find the letter that works for all four words, add it to each word, and then rearrange each set of letters to form a new word. For example, B can be added to LOSS, ONLY, AUTO and IRON to form SLOBS, NOBLY, ABOUT and ROBIN.

COMMON
LETTER

S A I L

G R E W

K E N T

G U R U

BANANARAMA

Each of the words below can be turned into another word on the list by changing one letter and then rearranging them all to form a new word. For example, REGIMENT can be turned into STEERING by changing the M to an S, so they would be a pair. How quickly can you find all the pairs?

<u>Pairs</u>

1. D U L C E T   ___ ___
2. H A N S O M   ___ ___
3. R A T I O S   ___ ___
4. B E L O N G   ___ ___
5. M E N I A L   ___ ___
6. G E N T L E
7. G O B L I N
8. M O N T H S
9. T R O I K A
10. T A L C E D
11. E A G L E T
12. L A Y M E N

BANANA CHIPS

Each set of letters below is arranged alphabetically, and the ? is in the correct alphabetical position. Figure out what letter the ? represents and rearrange the letters to spell a six-letter word. For example, in A?ENTV the ? could be an A, B, C, D or E. Here it represents a D, which can be combined with the other letters to spell ADVENT. The first letter is placed to get you started.

C C ? O T U

O ☐ ☐ ☐ ☐ ☐

A N P ? U W

U ☐ ☐ ☐ ☐ ☐

A G ? T U U

A ☐ ☐ ☐ ☐ ☐

A F M O ? T

F ☐ ☐ ☐ ☐ ☐

A E G ? P U

P ☐ ☐ ☐ ☐ ☐

A H N O ? Y

A ☐ ☐ ☐ ☐ ☐

B E E H ? Y

H ☐ ☐ ☐ ☐ ☐

A C D ? I N

C ☐ ☐ ☐ ☐ ☐

A B P ? S U

S ☐ ☐ ☐ ☐ ☐

B ? F I O R

F ☐ ☐ ☐ ☐ ☐

TOP BANANA

For each bunch below, rearrange the letters to form two intersecting words that fit into the corresponding grid.

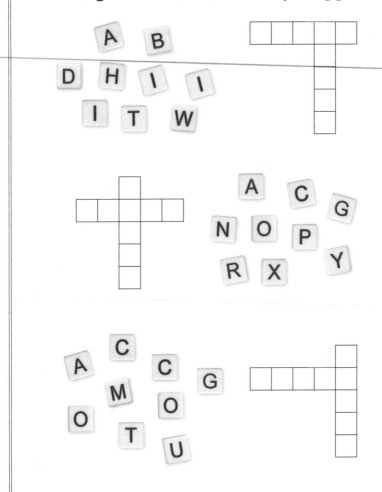

BANANA CRUNCH

Each set of 10 tiles below contains two common five-letter words. The letters of the first five-letter word are adjacent, but not in order. Find them and rearrange them to spell a word. Cross out those letters and imagine that the five remaining letters are now consecutive. These remaining letters can now be rearranged to spell the second word.

Example: GTIAKLPOTH. AKLPO can be rearranged into POLKA. That leaves GTITH, which can be rearranged into TIGHT.

ARCODRHFEM

YNABCCUIPS

NAUURAGNUL

AALLIFWERY

BANANA PUDDING

Each of the two-letter groups below may be extended both on the right and the left to form a six-letter word. Drawing from the tiles directly above each group, fill in the blanks to find the words as quickly as you can.

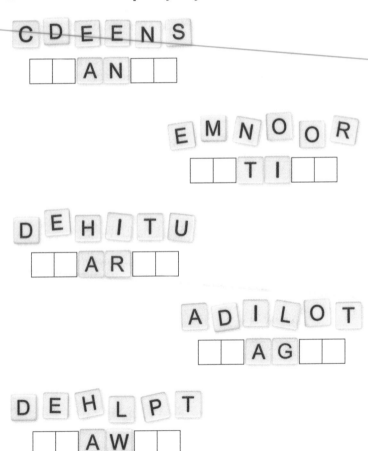

C D E E N S

☐ ☐ A N ☐ ☐

E M N O O R

☐ ☐ T I ☐ ☐

D E H I T U

☐ ☐ A R ☐ ☐

A D I L O T

☐ ☐ A G ☐ ☐

D E H L P T

☐ ☐ A W ☐ ☐

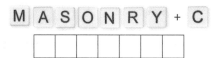

TOTALLY BANANAS

For each of the words below, replace one letter with the tile after the plus sign. Then rearrange the letters to form a 20th-century invention.

M A S O N R Y + C

R E S T A R T + O

S K Y L I T + N

G R O V E L + C

P R I Z E S + P

A W A R D + R

143

BANANA TREES

Use the 15 tiles in this bunch to create words that fit into the grids below. To get you started, a few tiles from the bunch have been placed in the grid. The BANANA BITES provide hints to help you solve each grid. Reuse the 15 tiles in the bunch for each grid.

1. BANANA BITE: One word means "to transport."

2. BANANA BITE: One word means "cheesy."

3. BANANA BITE: One word means "curved outward."

4. BANANA BITE: One word is a type of symbol.

BUNCH OF BANANAS

For each word or phrase below, rearrange the letters to spell two new words that can be used to describe groups of living things. For example, CURLED A BUNT can be rearranged to spell BAND (coyotes) and CULTURE (bacteria). The first letter of each word is placed to get you started.

BRIE   DEBT
T ☐ ☐ ☐ ☐   B ☐ ☐

DEEP   RIND
P ☐ ☐ ☐ ☐   D ☐ ☐

ANT   SPECK
N ☐ ☐ ☐   P ☐ ☐ ☐

MAY   PROD
A ☐ ☐ ☐   P ☐ ☐

MAY   BE   VET
B ☐ ☐ ☐   T ☐ ☐ ☐

EGGED   A   RAP   GAL
P ☐ ☐ ☐ ☐ ☐   G ☐ ☐ ☐ ☐ ☐

145

Rearrange the letters of each word below and place them in the blanks so that, together with the two letters that have already been placed, they form a new word.

M O L E

C _ _ _ Y

R O A D

P _ _ _ Y

M A N Y

D _ _ _ O

O P A L

U _ _ _ D

BANANA FILLING

Add an N to each of the words below and then rearrange the letters in each word to form a new six-letter word.

E D E M A

☐☐☐☐☐☐

L A T K E

☐☐☐☐☐☐

A V E R T

☐☐☐☐☐☐

F A I N T

☐☐☐☐☐☐

Using three of the tiles from the bunch on the left, fill in the blanks on the right to make a six-letter word that connects the grid.

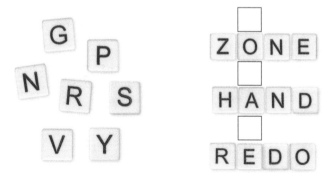

G
P
N
R S
V Y

☐
Z O N E
☐
H A N D
☐
R E D O

BANANA SHAKES

Each of the following six-letter sets can be rearranged to spell out a common word that either starts with FO **, HA , or SP _or_ ends with UM , UT , or UR . Find all the words as quickly as you can.**

A E N P T U
☐☐☐☐☐☐

G I O P S T
☐☐☐☐☐☐

D E O R U V
☐☐☐☐☐☐

A L N T U W
☐☐☐☐☐☐

A A H R S S
☐☐☐☐☐☐

A M P S S S
☐☐☐☐☐☐

C D I M T U
☐☐☐☐☐☐

F K L O S Y
☐☐☐☐☐☐

M O P S S U
☐☐☐☐☐☐

C C N O R U
☐☐☐☐☐☐

A H I N P T
☐☐☐☐☐☐

F H O R T U
☐☐☐☐☐☐

BANANA PEELS

There is <u>one letter</u> that when added to all of the four-letter words below can be used to form new five-letter words. Find the letter that works for all four words, add it to each word, and then rearrange each set of letters to form a new word. For example, B can be added to LOSS, ONLY, AUTO and IRON to form SLOBS, NOBLY, ABOUT and ROBIN.

COMMON
LETTER

YETI

DEAF

VIAL

NAYS

Each of the words below can be turned into another word on the list by changing one letter and then rearranging them all to form a new word. For example, REGIMENT can be turned into STEERING by changing the M to an S, so they would be a pair. How quickly can you find all the pairs?

Pairs

1. A D R I F T   ___ ___

2. S H O G U N   ___ ___

3. N I B B L E   ___ ___

4. E T C H E D   ___ ___

5. O I L I N G   ___ ___

6. B Y L I N E

7. U G S O M E

8. R A T I F Y

9. D E F E C T

10. G U A N O S

11. V I O L I N

12. G O L E M S

BANANA CHIPS

Each set of letters below is arranged alphabetically, and the
? is in the correct alphabetical position. Figure out what
letter the ? represents and rearrange the letters to spell
a six-letter word. For example, in A?ENTV the ? could be
an A, B, C, D or E. Here it represents a D, which can be
combined with the other letters to spell ADVENT. The first
letter is placed to get you started.

? E E M R Y

R ☐ ☐ ☐ ☐ ☐

I ? O P R V

I ☐ ☐ ☐ ☐ ☐

B E I ? N Y

B ☐ ☐ ☐ ☐ ☐

A E E ? L X

E ☐ ☐ ☐ ☐ ☐

B E L ? P U

P ☐ ☐ ☐ ☐ ☐

E G L L ? U

G ☐ ☐ ☐ ☐ ☐

A E ? M R V

M ☐ ☐ ☐ ☐ ☐

E E F ? T W

F ☐ ☐ ☐ ☐ ☐

? E F I O O

F ☐ ☐ ☐ ☐ ☐

B C G O ? Y

C ☐ ☐ ☐ ☐ ☐

TOP BANANA

For each bunch below, rearrange the letters to form two intersecting words that fit into the corresponding grid.

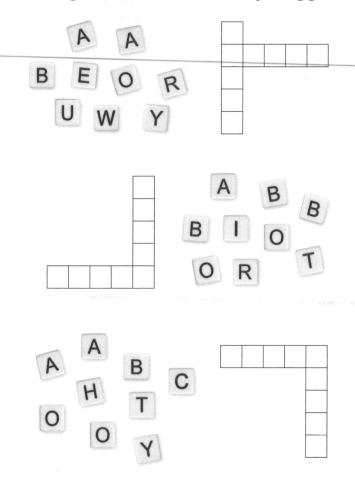

BANANA CRUNCH

Each set of 10 tiles below contains two common five-letter words. The letters of the first five-letter word are adjacent, but not in order. Find them and rearrange them to spell a word. Cross out those letters and imagine that the five remaining letters are now consecutive. These remaining letters can now be rearranged to spell the second word.

Example: GTIAKLPOTH. AKLPO can be rearranged into POLKA. That leaves GTITH, which can be rearranged into TIGHT.

L I G C A K A B U D

T D E E G I N O I T

P A A L N C V E E E

L G U L A H H L O E

BANANA PUDDING

Each of the two-letter groups below may be extended both on the right and the left to form a six-letter word. Drawing from the tiles directly above each group, fill in the blanks to find the words as quickly as you can.

C E E I M P

☐ ☐ A N ☐ ☐

C E E F N T

☐ ☐ L I ☐ ☐

B E H S T U

☐ ☐ A T ☐ ☐

A D E P R T

☐ ☐ U N ☐ ☐

D E G L O R

☐ ☐ U N ☐ ☐

TOTALLY BANANAS

For each of the words below, replace one letter with the tile after the plus sign. Then rearrange the letters to form the name of a famous fictional character.

T O A D + Y

☐ ☐ ☐ ☐

C L E A N + I

☐ ☐ ☐ ☐ ☐

M A N T R A + B

☐ ☐ ☐ ☐ ☐ ☐

R I N K + K

☐ ☐ ☐ ☐

M E T R I C + K

☐ ☐ ☐ ☐ ☐ ☐

F L A G M A N + D

☐ ☐ ☐ ☐ ☐ ☐ ☐

BANANA TREES

Use the 15 tiles in this bunch to create words that fit into the grids below. To get you started, a few tiles from the bunch have been placed in the grid. The BANANA BITES provide hints to help you solve each grid. Reuse the 15 tiles in the bunch for each grid.

2. BANANA BITE: One word means "a sign."

1. BANANA BITE: One word means "free of noise."

4. BANANA BITE: One word is something you chew on.

3. BANANA BITE: One word means "query."

BUNCH OF BANANAS

For each word or phrase below, rearrange the letters to spell two last names of co-starring actors. For example, **ONE MENTOR NAPS** can be rearranged to spell NEESON, PORTMAN ("Star Wars, Episode 1: The Phantom Menace"). The first letter of each word is placed to get you started.

I PELT TYCOON
C _ _ _ _ _ _   P _ _ _

B E G E T S   E R R O R
G _ _ _ _   R _ _ _ _ _ _

G A L S   C O O L E D   U S
D _ _ _ _ _ _   C _ _ _ _

S A G A   T E R R O R I S E
A _ _ _ _ _ _   R _ _ _ _ _

C U R E   R O O M I E S
C _ _ _ _ _   M _ _ _ _

L E G A L   B R E E D
B _ _ _   L _ _ _ _ _

157

ONE
BANANA

P U Z Z L E S

BANANA BITES

Rearrange the letters of each word below and place them in the blanks so that, together with the two letters that have already been placed, they form a new word.

T O R T E

L _ _ _ _ Y

T O W E D

L _ _ _ _ N

B L O A T

N _ _ _ _ E

S P O O N

S _ _ _ _ R

BANANA FILLING

Add a Y to each of the words below and then rearrange the letters in each word to form a new seven-letter word.

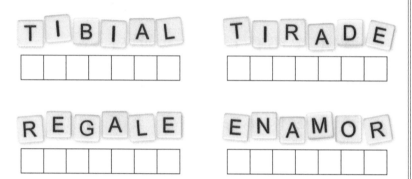

T I B I A L

[ ][ ][ ][ ][ ][ ][ ]

T I R A D E

[ ][ ][ ][ ][ ][ ][ ]

R E G A L E

[ ][ ][ ][ ][ ][ ][ ]

E N A M O R

[ ][ ][ ][ ][ ][ ][ ]

Using four of the tiles from the bunch on the left, fill in the blanks on the right to make a seven-letter word that connects the grid.

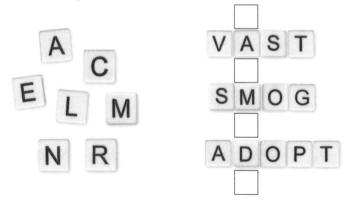

161

BANANA SHAKES

Each of the following six-letter sets can be rearranged to spell out a common word that either starts with B **,** D **, or** G **and/or ends with** A **,** R **, or** T **. Find all the words as quickly as you can.**

A A B D L L

A E G I M N

A B E K N R

A B E K S T

A A D H I L

A E G L L Y

C D E E F T

A D F G L Y

A A D E G N

A C D D E E

A B B M O O

A E N R S W

BANANA PEELS

There is <u>one letter</u> that when added to all of the five-letter words below can be used to form new six-letter words. Find the letter that works for all four words, add it to each word, and then rearrange each set of letters to form a new word. For example, L can be added to ROADS, WEARY, EPICS and GONER to form DORSAL, LAWYER, SPLICE and LONGER.

COMMON
LETTER

C R A N E

A C U T E

A N T I C

K E N O S

BANANARAMA

Each of the words below can be turned into another word on the list by changing one letter and then rearranging them all to form a new word. For example, REGIMENT can be turned into STEERING by changing the M to an S, so they would be a pair. How quickly can you find all the pairs?

Pairs

1. A R C H F O E   ___ ___

2. F I N I C A L   ___ ___

3. F U S A R I A   ___ ___

4. B E S I E G E   ___ ___

5. P I G T A I L   ___ ___

6. M O D E S T Y

7. C H O L E R A

8. T I L A P I A

9. I N F L I C T

10. E L E G I E S

11. S O M E D A Y

12. S A U R I A N

BANANA CHIPS

Each set of letters below is arranged alphabetically, and the
? is in the correct alphabetical position. Figure out what
letter the ? represents and rearrange the letters to spell
a six-letter word. For example, in A?ENTV the ? could be
an A, B, C, D or E. Here it represents a D, which can be
combined with the other letters to spell ADVENT. The last
letter is placed to get you started.

A D I ? R W

					D

E E I ? V V

					E

B D N O ? Y

					Y

E H O ? T Y

					Y

C F ? I N O

					N

D ? I O R R

					D

A ? M M N U

					M

A O O T T ?

					O

D I O ? T U

					O

? E E F O R

					E

TOP BANANA

For each bunch below, rearrange the letters to form two intersecting words that fit into the corresponding grid.

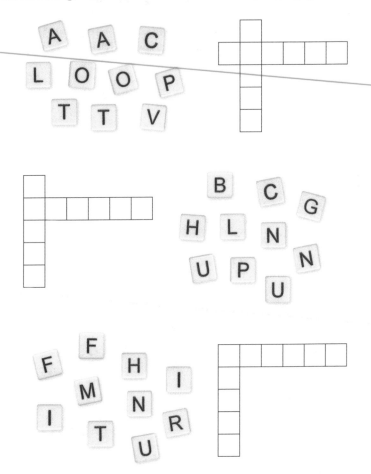

BANANA CRUNCH

Each set of 12 tiles below contains two common six-letter words. The letters of the first six-letter word are adjacent, but not in order. Find them and rearrange them to spell a word. Cross out those letters and imagine that the six remaining letters are now consecutive. These remaining letters can now be rearranged to spell the second word.

Example: ALCUERHTLPEA. UERHTL can be rearranged into HURTLE. That leaves ALCPEA, which can be rearranged into PALACE.

E H E B S U U B R B L D

L O G P E I T P C B E T

F E R R U T I E E R H S

S M U I N N E T T A K N

BANANA PUDDING

Each of the two-letter groups below may be extended both on the right and the left to form a six-letter word. Drawing from the tiles directly above each group, fill in the blanks to find the words as quickly as you can.

A C D E M P U

☐ ☐ L O ☐ ☐

C L M N O P T

☐ ☐ B A ☐ ☐

A B E G N T U

☐ ☐ L O ☐ ☐

G H I N R T U

☐ ☐ F A ☐ ☐

A C D E O P R

☐ ☐ L A ☐ ☐

TOTALLY BANANAS

For each of the words below, replace one letter with the tile after the plus sign. Then rearrange the letters to form an animal.

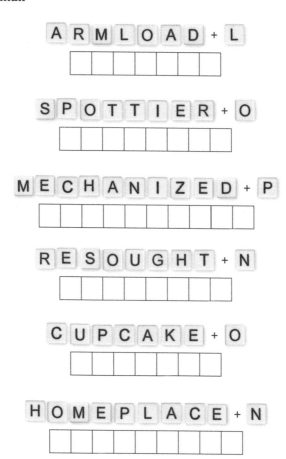

A R M L O A D + L

S P O T T I E R + O

M E C H A N I Z E D + P

R E S O U G H T + N

C U P C A K E + O

H O M E P L A C E + N

BANANA TREES

Use the 15 tiles in this bunch to create words that fit into the grids below. To get you started, a few tiles from the bunch have been placed in the grid. Reuse the 15 tiles in the bunch for each grid.

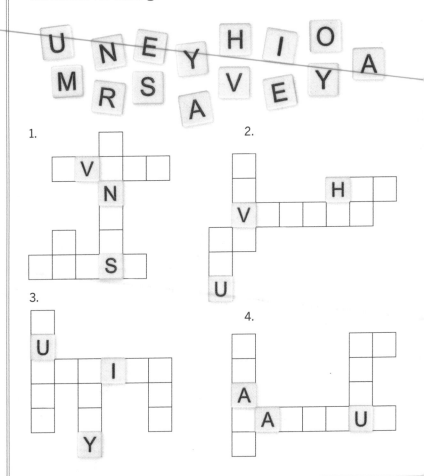

BUNCH OF BANANAS

For each word or phrase below, rearrange the letters to spell two new words that are synonyms. For example, **WIZARD PEAR** can be rearranged to spell **AWARD, PRIZE**. The last letter of each word is placed to get you started.

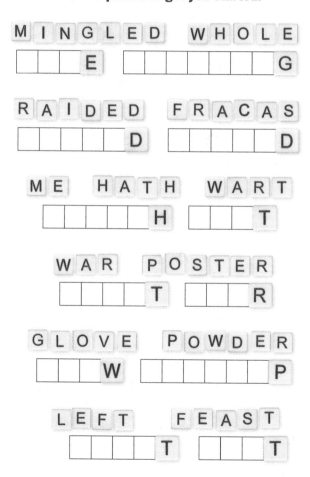

MINGLED   WHOLE
□ □ □ E □   □ □ □ □ □ □ G

RAIDED   FRACAS
□ □ □ □ □ D   □ □ □ □ D

ME HATH WART
□ □ □ □ □ H   □ □ □ T

WAR POSTER
□ □ □ □ T   □ □ □ R

GLOVE POWDER
□ □ □ W   □ □ □ □ □ P

LEFT FEAST
□ □ □ □ T   □ □ T

BANANA BITES

Rearrange the letters of each word below and place them in the blanks so that, together with the two letters that have already been placed, they form a new word.

R A T I O

P _ _ _ _ _ T

B I T E S

O _ _ _ _ _ Y

L A B O R

E _ _ _ _ E

A U R I C

H _ _ _ _ T

BANANA FILLING

Add an R to each of the words below and then rearrange
the letters in each word to form a new seven-letter word.

N I E C E S

P A E O N S

P R A Y E D

F A M I N E

Using four of the tiles from the bunch on the left, fill in
the blanks on the right to make a seven-letter word that
connects the grid.

A I
H
L P
T U

A N D

H E P

U S E

BANANA SHAKES

Each of the following six-letter sets can be rearranged to spell out a common word that either starts with E, M, or S and/or ends with M, T, or Y. Find all the words as quickly as you can.

A B G I M T
☐☐☐☐☐☐

E M M N O T
☐☐☐☐☐☐

C E R S W Y
☐☐☐☐☐☐

D E E M O W
☐☐☐☐☐☐

A B E K M R
☐☐☐☐☐☐

A B E T U Y
☐☐☐☐☐☐

C K M O P U
☐☐☐☐☐☐

A C E G L Y
☐☐☐☐☐☐

E H I L M U
☐☐☐☐☐☐

E M M S U U
☐☐☐☐☐☐

C H I N S T
☐☐☐☐☐☐

C D E E N O
☐☐☐☐☐☐

BANANA PEELS

There is <u>one letter</u> that when added to all of the five-letter words below can be used to form new six-letter words. Find the letter that works for all four words, add it to each word, and then rearrange each set of letters to form a new word. For example, L can be added to ROADS, WEARY, EPICS and GONER to form DORSAL, LAWYER, SPLICE and LONGER.

COMMON
LETTER

[ ]

S L U E S

[ ][ ][ ][ ][ ][ ]

A P I S H

[ ][ ][ ][ ][ ][ ]

C O R A L

[ ][ ][ ][ ][ ][ ]

N A M E D

[ ][ ][ ][ ][ ][ ]

BANANARAMA

Each of the words below can be turned into another word on the list by changing one letter and then rearranging them all to form a new word. For example, REGIMENT can be turned into STEERING by changing the M to an S, so they would be a pair. How quickly can you find all the pairs?

1. B U L L D O G

2. A C E T O N E

3. S E A B A G S

4. P O T E N C E

5. G L O B U L E

6. O A R L I K E

7. N O N D R U G

8. M I S B I A S

9. A I R H O L E

10. P A S S A G E

11. R U N D O W N

12. S A S H I M I

Pairs

___ ___

___ ___

___ ___

___ ___

___ ___

BANANA CHIPS

Each set of letters below is arranged alphabetically, and the ? is in the correct alphabetical position. Figure out what letter the ? represents and rearrange the letters to spell a six-letter word. For example, in A?ENTV the ? could be an A, B, C, D or E. Here it represents a D, which can be combined with the other letters to spell ADVENT. The last letter is placed to get you started.

D G ? O O T

| | | | | | G |

A ? N T U U

| | | | | | N |

? E K N O Y

| | | | | | Y |

A K ? P R U

| | | | | | P |

A L L ? R U

| | | | | | L |

D I ? R T U

| | | | | | D |

B ? O O R T

| | | | | | T |

E F I I N ?

| | | | | | E |

E E H R ? Y

| | | | | | Y |

A ? I J S W

| | | | | | W |

TOP BANANA

For each bunch below, rearrange the letters to form two
intersecting words that fit into the corresponding grid.

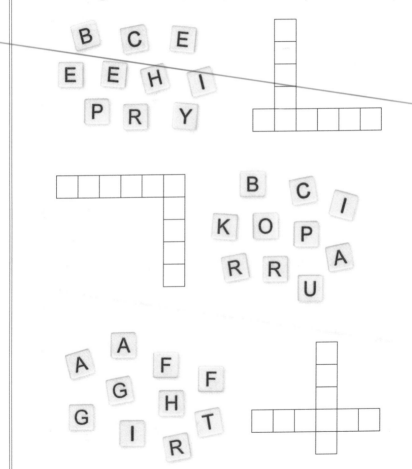

BANANA CRUNCH

Each set of 12 tiles below contains two common six-letter words. The letters of the first six-letter word are adjacent, but not in order. Find them and rearrange them to spell a word. Cross out those letters and imagine that the six remaining letters are now consecutive. These remaining letters can now be rearranged to spell the second word.

Example: ALCUERHTLPEA. UERHTL can be rearranged into HURTLE. That leaves ALCPEA, which can be rearranged into PALACE.

F A E G I S V C O T A R

R A T A U Y N S E K M E

L O M A L F E E C N U M

A T R A H H R O O M O L

BANANA PUDDING

Each of the two-letter groups below may be extended both on the right and the left to form a six-letter word. Drawing from the tiles directly above each group, fill in the blanks to find the words as quickly as you can.

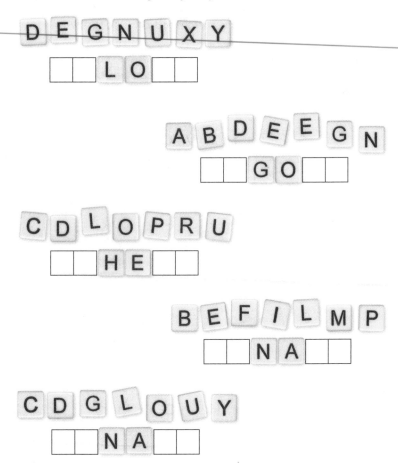

D E G N U X Y

⬜ ⬜ L O ⬜ ⬜

A B D E E G N

⬜ ⬜ G O ⬜ ⬜

C D L O P R U

⬜ ⬜ H E ⬜ ⬜

B E F I L M P

⬜ ⬜ N A ⬜ ⬜

C D G L O U Y

⬜ ⬜ N A ⬜ ⬜

TOTALLY BANANAS

For each of the words below, replace one letter with the tile after the plus sign. Then rearrange the letters to form a type of shape.

E M I G R A N T + L

☐ ☐ ☐ ☐ ☐ ☐ ☐ ☐

C O N C R E T E + S

☐ ☐ ☐ ☐ ☐ ☐ ☐ ☐

G E N E T I C A L + R

☐ ☐ ☐ ☐ ☐ ☐ ☐ ☐ ☐

P R E D A T I O N + Z

☐ ☐ ☐ ☐ ☐ ☐ ☐ ☐

P A G E A N T R Y + M

☐ ☐ ☐ ☐ ☐ ☐ ☐ ☐ ☐

S O R G H U M + B

☐ ☐ ☐ ☐ ☐ ☐ ☐

BANANA TREES

Use the 15 tiles in this bunch to create words that fit into the grids below. To get you started, a few tiles from the bunch have been placed in the grid. Reuse the 15 tiles in the bunch for each grid.

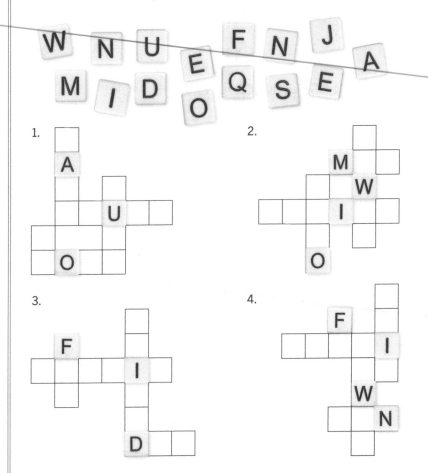

BUNCH OF BANANAS

For each word or phrase below, rearrange the letters to spell two things that are green. For example, AGILE LOCO CRAB can be rearranged to spell BROCCOLI, ALGAE. The last letter of each word is placed to get you started.

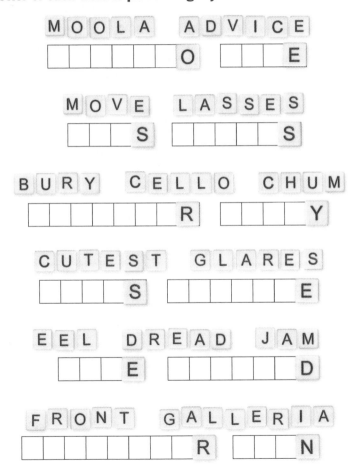

MOOLA   ADVICE

☐ ☐ ☐ ☐ ☐ O   ☐ ☐ ☐ E

MOVE   LASSES

☐ ☐ ☐ S   ☐ ☐ ☐ ☐ S

BURY   CELLO   CHUM

☐ ☐ ☐ ☐ ☐ ☐ R   ☐ ☐ ☐ Y

CUTEST   GLARES

☐ ☐ ☐ ☐ S   ☐ ☐ ☐ ☐ ☐ E

EEL   DREAD   JAM

☐ ☐ ☐ E   ☐ ☐ ☐ ☐ ☐ D

FRONT   GALLERIA

☐ ☐ ☐ ☐ ☐ ☐ ☐ ☐ R   ☐ ☐ N

BANANA BITES

Rearrange the letters of each word below and place them in the blanks so that, together with the two letters that have already been placed, they form a new word.

C O I N S

I _ _ _ _ R

P R E E N

S _ _ _ _ T

P R I O R

A _ _ _ _ T

E A T E N

B _ _ _ _ H

BANANA FILLING

Add a W to each of the words below and then rearrange the letters in each word to form a new seven-letter word.

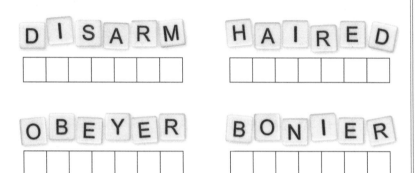

D I S A R M

H A I R E D

O B E Y E R

B O N I E R

Using four of the tiles from the bunch on the left, fill in the blanks on the right to make a seven-letter word that connects the grid.

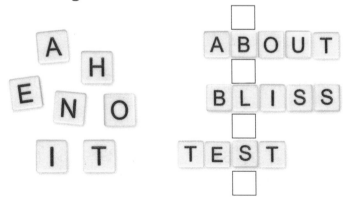

A H E N O I T

A B O U T
B L I S S
T E S T

BANANA SHAKES

Each of the following six-letter sets can be rearranged to spell out a common word that either starts with G, P, or R and/or ends with A, N, or T. Find all the words as quickly as you can.

A A M N R T

A N P R T Y

C L M N O U

A D M O R R

E E F S T W

E I M P R T

A C N O R Y

D E E G N R

A D I R S U

A A E N S U

E G I N S U

D E G I S T

186

BANANA PEELS

There is <u>one letter</u> that when added to all of the five-letter words below can be used to form new six-letter words. Find the letter that works for all four words, add it to each word, and then rearrange each set of letters to form a new word. For example, L can be added to ROADS, WEARY, EPICS and GONER to form DORSAL, LAWYER, SPLICE and LONGER.

COMMON
LETTER

F I L T H

T I P S Y

W A N T S

H I D E S

BANANARAMA

Each of the words below can be turned into another word on the list by changing one letter and then rearranging them all to form a new word. For example, REGIMENT can be turned into STEERING by changing the M to an S, so they would be a pair. How quickly can you find all the pairs?

Pairs

1. MATADOR

_____ _____

2. CHAPATI

_____ _____

3. ROSEBUD

_____ _____

4. PLASTIC

_____ _____

5. WETLAND

_____ _____

6. NARCOMA

7. OVERDUB

8. ITALICS

9. TALONED

10. STARDOM

11. HAIRCAP

12. OCARINA

BANANA CHIPS

Each set of letters below is arranged alphabetically, and the
? is in the correct alphabetical position. Figure out what
letter the ? represents and rearrange the letters to spell
a six-letter word. For example, in A?ENTV the ? could be
an A, B, C, D or E. Here it represents a D, which can be
combined with the other letters to spell ADVENT. The last
letter is placed to get you started.

E I I ? R X
| | | | | | R |

B E E ? M M
| | | | | | M |

D I M O ? W
| | | | | | M |

A B ? K R Y
| | | | | | Y |

E E E G N ?
| | | | | | E |

C C N ? R U
| | | | | | R |

D E ? T U Y
| | | | | | Y |

? E O S U X
| | | | | | S |

A E G I ? O
| | | | | | E |

A D L L ? R
| | | | | | R |

189

TOP BANANA

For each bunch below, rearrange the letters to form two intersecting words that fit into the corresponding grid.

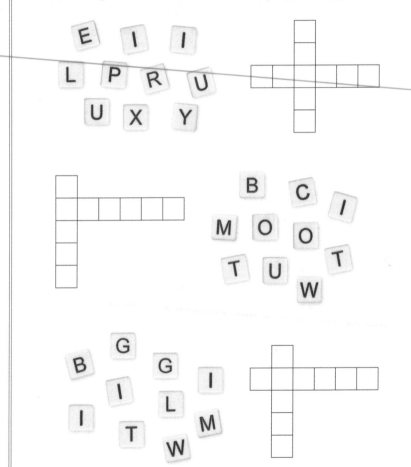

BANANA CRUNCH

Each set of 12 tiles below contains two common six-letter words. The letters of the first six-letter word are adjacent, but not in order. Find them and rearrange them to spell a word. Cross out those letters and imagine that the six remaining letters are now consecutive. These remaining letters can now be rearranged to spell the second word.

Example: ALCUERHTLPEA. UERHTL can be rearranged into HURTLE. That leaves ALCPEA, which can be rearranged into PALACE.

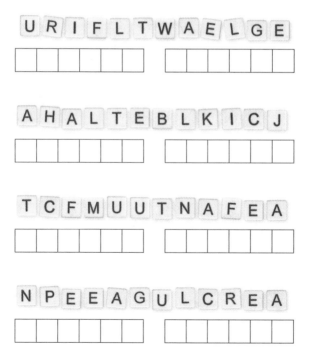

U R I F L T W A E L G E

A H A L T E B L K I C J

T C F M U U T N A F E A

N P E E A G U L C R E A

BANANA PUDDING

Each of the two-letter groups below may be extended both on the right and the left to form a six-letter word. Drawing from the tiles directly above each group, fill in the blanks to find the words as quickly as you can.

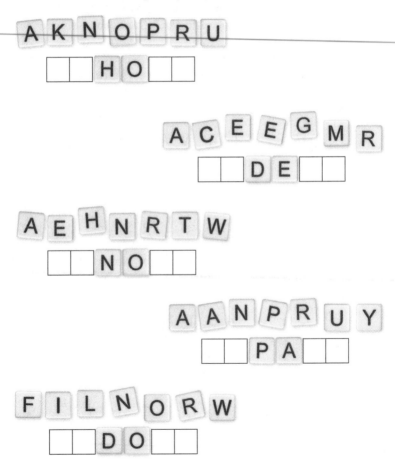

A K N O P R U

☐ ☐ H O ☐ ☐

A C E E G M R

☐ ☐ D E ☐ ☐

A E H N R T W

☐ ☐ N O ☐ ☐

A A N P R U Y

☐ ☐ P A ☐ ☐

F I L N O R W

☐ ☐ D O ☐ ☐

TOTALLY BANANAS

For each of the words below, replace one letter with the tile after the plus sign. Then rearrange the letters to form a popular board game.

OLYMPIADS + C

NUMERIC + A

IMPORTANCY + I

STAMMERING + D

BIATHLETES + P

POMOLOGY + N

BANANA TREES

Use the 15 tiles in this bunch to create words that fit into the grids below. To get you started, a few tiles from the bunch have been placed in the grid. Reuse the 15 tiles in the bunch for each grid.

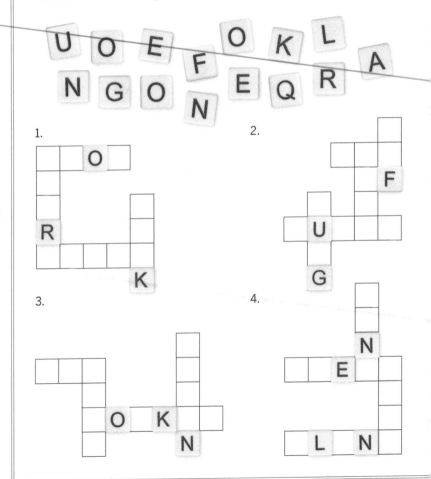

BUNCH OF BANANAS

For each word or phrase below, rearrange the letters to spell two new words that can both be combined with the suffix –BALL to form a compound word. For example, SOD DOWN can be rearranged to spell ODD (ball) and SNOW (ball). The last letter of each word is placed to get you started.

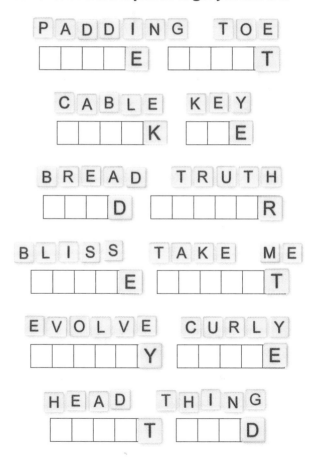

PADDING   TOE

[ ][ ][ ][ ][ ][E]   [ ][ ][ ][ ][ ][T]

CABLE   KEY

[ ][ ][ ][ ][ ][K]   [ ][ ][E]

BREAD   TRUTH

[ ][ ][ ][ ][D]   [ ][ ][ ][ ][ ][R]

BLISS   TAKE ME

[ ][ ][ ][ ][ ][E]   [ ][ ][ ][ ][ ][ ][T]

EVOLVE   CURLY

[ ][ ][ ][ ][ ][ ][Y]   [ ][ ][ ][ ][E]

HEAD   THING

[ ][ ][ ][ ][T]   [ ][ ][ ][ ][D]

BANANA BITES

Rearrange the letters of each word below and place them in the blanks so that, together with the two letters that have already been placed, they form a new word.

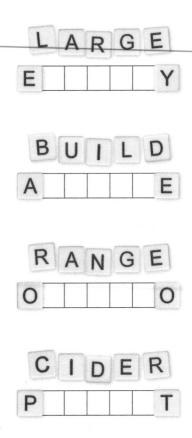

L A R G E
E _ _ _ _ _ Y

B U I L D
A _ _ _ _ _ E

R A N G E
O _ _ _ _ _ O

C I D E R
P _ _ _ _ _ T

BANANA FILLING

Add a U to each of the words below and then rearrange the letters in each word to form a new seven-letter word.

B O T A N Y

C L A I M S

L O C A L S

C A R R O T

Using four of the tiles from the bunch on the left, fill in the blanks on the right to make a seven-letter word that connects the grid.

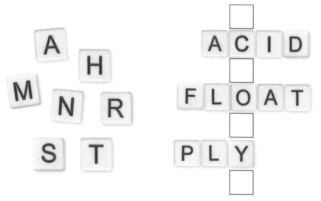

A C I D

F L O A T

P L Y

BANANA SHAKES

Each of the following six-letter sets can be rearranged to spell out a common word that either starts with `A`, `E`, **or** `I` <u>**and/or**</u> **ends with** `E`, `H`, **or** `W`**. Find all the words as quickly as you can.**

`B` `C` `E` `I` `O` `X`

☐☐☐☐☐☐

`C` `E` `E` `E` `F` `L`

☐☐☐☐☐☐

`D` `E` `I` `L` `M` `W`

☐☐☐☐☐☐

`E` `G` `H` `I` `L` `S`

☐☐☐☐☐☐

`A` `B` `H` `M` `S` `U`

☐☐☐☐☐☐

`E` `E` `H` `I` `R` `T`

☐☐☐☐☐☐

`H` `I` `L` `O` `P` `S`

☐☐☐☐☐☐

`C` `E` `I` `I` `L` `T`

☐☐☐☐☐☐

`A` `E` `N` `N` `O` `Y`

☐☐☐☐☐☐

`A` `E` `I` `R` `R` `V`

☐☐☐☐☐☐

`E` `I` `M` `M` `N` `U`

☐☐☐☐☐☐

`E` `F` `L` `L` `O` `W`

☐☐☐☐☐☐

There is <u>one letter</u> that when added to all of the five-letter words below can be used to form new six-letter words. Find the letter that works for all four words, add it to each word, and then rearrange each set of letters to form a new word. For example, L can be added to ROADS, WEARY, EPICS and GONER to form DORSAL, LAWYER, SPLICE and LONGER.

COMMON
LETTER

D U C A T

B O A R S

H E A V E

S P A Y S

BANANARAMA

Each of the words below can be turned into another word on the list by changing one letter and then rearranging them all to form a new word. For example, REGIMENT can be turned into STEERING by changing the M to an S, so they would be a pair. How quickly can you find all the pairs?

Pairs

1. B A S M A T I ___ ___

2. R O U L A D E ___ ___

3. S C A B I E S — —

4. A C T U A R Y ___ ___

5. T A N G R A M — —

6. C H I T L I N

7. A L F R E D O

8. A T A V I S M

9. T R U A N C Y

10. M A G E N T A

11. S E A S I C K

12. C H I A N T I

BANANA CHIPS

Each set of letters below is arranged alphabetically, and the ? is in the correct alphabetical position. Figure out what letter the ? represents and rearrange the letters to spell a six-letter word. For example, in A?ENTV the ? could be an A, B, C, D or E. Here it represents a D, which can be combined with the other letters to spell ADVENT. The last letter is placed to get you started.

C C I ? N P

					C

I ? R U T Y

					Y

E ? O O S V

					S

B C H I O ?

					C

? D E I P T

					T

A B C L ? T

					T

A A C I R ?

					R

? D E O U Y

					D

A F I N R ?

					R

A B E ? O Z

					O

For each bunch below, rearrange the letters to form two intersecting words that fit into the corresponding grid.

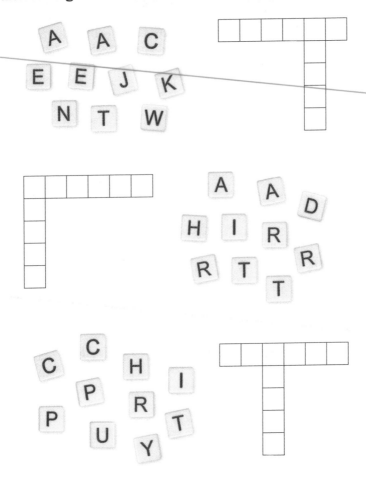

BANANA CRUNCH

Each set of 12 tiles below contains two common six-letter words. The letters of the first six-letter word are adjacent, but not in order. Find them and rearrange them to spell a word. Cross out those letters and imagine that the six remaining letters are now consecutive. These remaining letters can now be rearranged to spell the second word.

Example: ALCUERHTLPEA. UERHTL can be rearranged into HURTLE. That leaves ALCPEA, which can be rearranged into PALACE.

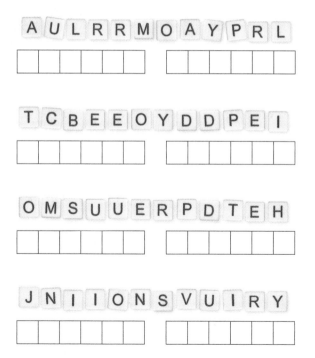

A U L R R M O A Y P R L

T C B E E O Y D D P E I

O M S U U E R P D T E H

J N I I O N S V U I R Y

BANANA PUDDING

Each of the two-letter groups below may be extended both on the right and the left to form a six-letter word. Drawing from the tiles directly above each group, fill in the blanks to find the words as quickly as you can.

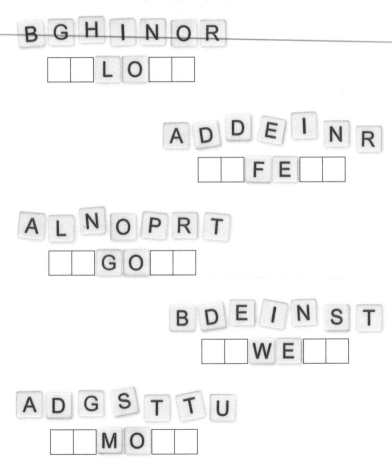

B G H I N O R
☐ ☐ L O ☐ ☐

A D D E I N R
☐ ☐ F E ☐ ☐

A L N O P R T
☐ ☐ G O ☐ ☐

B D E I N S T
☐ ☐ W E ☐ ☐

A D G S T T U
☐ ☐ M O ☐ ☐

TOTALLY BANANAS

For each of the words below, replace one letter with the
tile after the plus sign. Then rearrange the letters to form
something found in space.

ENRAPT + L

☐☐☐☐☐☐

MOTEL + C

☐☐☐☐☐

BROADEST + I

☐☐☐☐☐☐☐

CAVERNOUS + P

☐☐☐☐☐☐☐☐

LEGISLATE + T

☐☐☐☐☐☐☐☐

QUARTS + A

☐☐☐☐☐☐

BANANA TREES

Use the 15 tiles in this bunch to create words that fit into the grids below. To get you started, a few tiles from the bunch have been placed in the grid. Reuse the 15 tiles in the bunch for each grid.

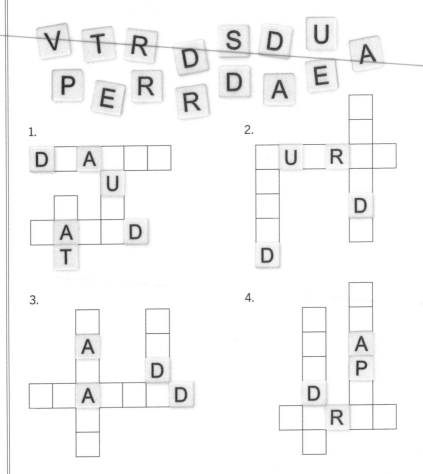

BUNCH OF BANANAS

For each word or phrase below, rearrange the letters to spell two new words that are opposites in meaning. For example, WEAR CAPE can be rearranged to spell WAR, PEACE. The last letter of each word is placed to get you started.

BUDDY

| | | | | D |

LOITERS

| | | | | | | Y |

PREVUE

| | | T | | |

TOXINS

| | | | | | | S |

FUEL

| | | | E |

RATES

| | | | | E |

DREAM

| | | D |

DOVE

| | | | | | E |

ANKLES

| | | | | | N |

TILT

| | | | K |

DO ROLE

| | | | | R |

FARE WELL

| | | | | | | R |

Rearrange the letters of each word below and place them in the blanks so that, together with the two letters that have already been placed, they form a new word.

N A M E R

G _ _ _ _ T

E N N U I

G _ _ _ _ E

W R O T E

N _ _ _ _ K

T A N G O

M _ _ _ _ E

BANANA FILLING

Add an S to each of the words below and then rearrange the letters in each word to form a new seven-letter word.

Using four of the tiles from the bunch on the left, fill in the blanks on the right to make a seven-letter word that connects the grid.

BANANA SHAKES

Each of the following six-letter sets can be rearranged to spell out a common word that either starts with W **,** M **, or** A **and/or ends with** A **,** C **, or** N **. Find all the words as quickly as you can.**

A I M M O S

C E I M R T

A E E H N V

A A R S T Y

A H M R T W

A M O R S S

C N O O P U

A D N O R U

C E I O T X

A E L L M T

A G I M S T

D E I O R W

BANANA PEELS

There is <u>one letter</u> that when added to all of the five-letter words below can be used to form new six-letter words. Find the letter that works for all four words, add it to each word, and then rearrange each set of letters to form a new word. For example, L can be added to ROADS, WEARY, EPICS and GONER to form DORSAL, LAWYER, SPLICE and LONGER.

COMMON
LETTER

H A I R S

I N L A Y

T O R I C

S T E E L

BANANARAMA

Each of the words below can be turned into another word on the list by changing one letter and then rearranging them all to form a new word. For example, REGIMENT can be turned into STEERING by changing the M to an S, so they would be a pair. How quickly can you find all the pairs?

1. P A T I E N T

2. M A G I C A L

3. B A N D A G E

4. P E A N U T S

5. L O C A T O R

6. C U L P R I T

7. B E A N B A G

8. A C C L A I M

9. T I N T Y P E

10. P I C T U R E

11. C A R P O O L

12. U N S T R A P

Pairs

___ ___

___ ___

___ ___

___ ___

___ ___

___ ___

BANANA CHIPS

Each set of letters below is arranged alphabetically, and the ? is in the correct alphabetical position. Figure out what letter the ? represents and rearrange the letters to spell a six-letter word. For example, in A?ENTV the ? could be an A, B, C, D or E. Here it represents a D, which can be combined with the other letters to spell ADVENT. The last letter is placed to get you started.

E E F G R ?

| | | | | | E |

C G H I O ?

| | | | | | C |

D I ? N O O

| | | | | | O |

E E ? L V W

| | | | | | L |

E E G ? N O

| | | | | | E |

? I L L W Y

| | | | | | Y |

C ? K O O U

| | | | | | O |

? L N U U Y

| | | | | | Y |

A I L ? V Y

| | | | | | Y |

B E F L ? Y

| | | | | | Y |

TOP BANANA

For each bunch below, rearrange the letters to form two intersecting words that fit into the corresponding grid.

BANANA CRUNCH

Each set of 12 tiles below contains two common six-letter words. The letters of the first six-letter word are adjacent, but not in order. Find them and rearrange them to spell a word. Cross out those letters and imagine that the six remaining letters are now consecutive. These remaining letters can now be rearranged to spell the second word.

Example: **ALCUERHTLPEA. UERHTL** can be rearranged into **HURTLE.** That leaves **ALCPEA,** which can be rearranged into **PALACE.**

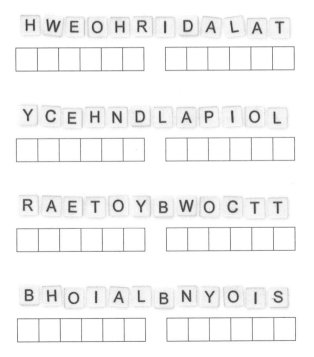

H W E O H R I D A L A T

Y C E H N D L A P I O L

R A E T O Y B W O C T T

B H O I A L B N Y O I S

BANANA PUDDING

Each of the two-letter groups below may be extended both on the right and the left to form a six-letter word. Drawing from the tiles directly above each group, fill in the blanks to find the words as quickly as you can.

A E E H P R S

☐ ☐ D O ☐ ☐

A B D E P R U

☐ ☐ M I ☐ ☐

A A D E L M P

☐ ☐ N U ☐ ☐

A N O S T T Y

☐ ☐ P I ☐ ☐

D I I N R T V

☐ ☐ L A ☐ ☐

TOTALLY BANANAS

For each of the words below, replace one letter with the tile after the plus sign. Then rearrange the letters to form a type of artist.

C E R T A I N + P

A S T R O N O M I C + T

S U B L I T T O R A L + R

D I S A G R E E + N

C O R R U P T S + L

C A T H A R T I C + E

BANANA TREES

Use the 15 tiles in this bunch to create words that fit into the grids below. To get you started, a few tiles from the bunch have been placed in the grid. Reuse the 15 tiles in the bunch for each grid.

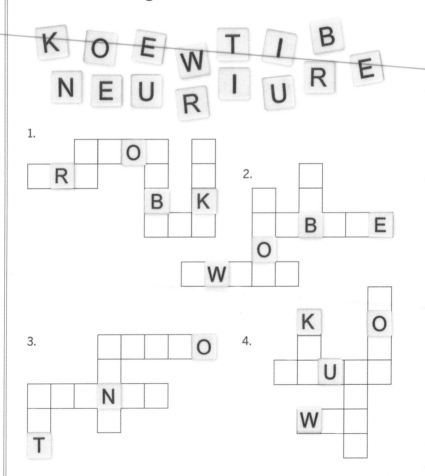

BUNCH OF BANANAS

For each word or phrase below, rearrange the letters to spell two new words that represent a pair of people who work together. For example, JULY RAGWEED can be rearranged to spell JUDGE, LAWYER. The last letter of each word is placed to get you started.

TEENAGE
[ ] [ ] [ ] [ ] [ ] [ ] R

SPARK
[ ] [ ] [ ] [ ] T

PECCARY
[ ] [ ] [ ] [ ] [ ] [ ] R

HALO
[ ] [ ] [ ] H

HIS PROP
[ ] [ ] [ ] [ ] [ ] [ ] T

BITES
[ ] [ ] [ ] [ ] P

CINEMA
[ ] [ ] [ ] [ ] [ ] [ ] N

PROF
[ ] P

CARING
[ ] [ ] [ ] [ ] [ ] R

SENDER
[ ] [ ] [ ] [ ] [ ] R

CAT
[ ] [ ] R

RECORD RIOT
[ ] [ ] [ ] [ ] [ ] [ ] [ ] R

BANANA BITES

Rearrange the letters of each word below and place them in the blanks so that, together with the two letters that have already been placed, they form a new word.

W O O L Y

P _ _ _ _ D

G N A R L

W _ _ _ _ E

H A I R S

W _ _ _ _ P

N O V E L

S _ _ _ _ T

BANANA FILLING

Add a P to each of the words below and then rearrange the letters in each word to form a new seven-letter word.

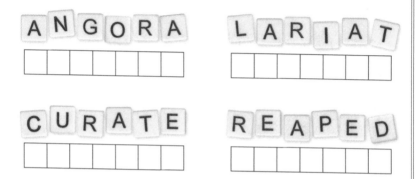

A N G O R A

L A R I A T

C U R A T E

R E A P E D

Using four of the tiles from the bunch on the left, fill in the blanks on the right to make a seven-letter word that connects the grid.

C
E
N
R V
S Y

P A R T

W I N

S T O P

BANANA SHAKES

Each of the following six-letter sets can be rearranged to spell out a common word that either starts with B, P, **or** T **and/or ends with** L, O, **or** R. **Find all the words as quickly as you can.**

ELMMPU

ACCILO

ABDINT

EEFLNN

AILMPR

EFORRV

EEMPRT

CEIKTT

EGLORV

BELOOR

DEHIRT

BEEFOR

BANANA PEELS

There is <u>one letter</u> that when added to all of the five-letter words below can be used to form new six-letter words. Find the letter that works for all four words, add it to each word, and then rearrange each set of letters to form a new word. For example, L can be added to ROADS, WEARY, EPICS and GONER to form DORSAL, LAWYER, SPLICE and LONGER.

COMMON
LETTER

[ ]

V A R I A

[ ][ ][ ][ ][ ][ ]

B A L M Y

[ ][ ][ ][ ][ ][ ]

E R A S E

[ ][ ][ ][ ][ ][ ]

L A T K E

[ ][ ][ ][ ][ ][ ]

BANANARAMA

Each of the words below can be turned into another word on the list by changing one letter and then rearranging them all to form a new word. For example, REGIMENT can be turned into STEERING by changing the M to an S, so they would be a pair. How quickly can you find all the pairs?

		Pairs
1.	D I A G R A M	___ ___
2.	D I L A T O R	___ ___
3.	G E L A T I N	___ ___
4.	F I F T E E N	___ ___
5.	S K I W E A R	___ ___
6.	B A R M A I D	
7.	T R I F O L D	
8.	H A D R O N S	
9.	I N F L A T E	
10.	B E N E F I T	
11.	S E M I R A W	
12.	S A N D H O G	

224

BANANA CHIPS

Each set of letters below is arranged alphabetically, and the
? is in the correct alphabetical position. Figure out what
letter the ? represents and rearrange the letters to spell
a six-letter word. For example, in A?ENTV the ? could be
an A, B, C, D or E. Here it represents a D, which can be
combined with the other letters to spell ADVENT. The last
letter is placed to get you started.

A ? E T U Y
[ ][ ][ ][ ][ ][Y]

A A ? I N U
[ ][ ][ ][ ][ ][A]

A H O ? T T
[ ][ ][ ][ ][ ][T]

D I I L ? U
[ ][ ][ ][ ][ ][D]

? E E G G N
[ ][ ][ ][ ][ ][E]

A E F ? S Y
[ ][ ][ ][ ][ ][Y]

D N R ? U Y
[ ][ ][ ][ ][ ][Y]

G H N ? U Y
[ ][ ][ ][ ][ ][Y]

F ? N S U U
[ ][ ][ ][ ][ ][S]

E E ? I N N
[ ][ ][ ][ ][ ][E]

TOP BANANA

**For each bunch below, rearrange the letters to form two
intersecting words that fit into the corresponding grid.**

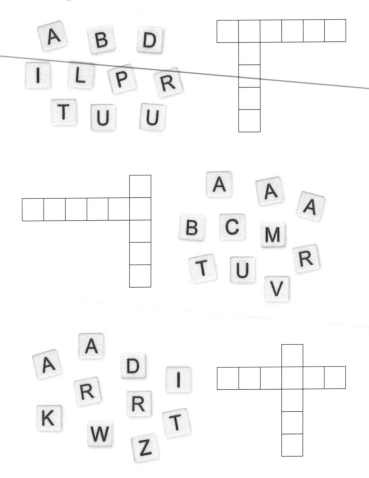

BANANA CRUNCH

Each set of 12 tiles below contains two common six-letter words. The letters of the first six-letter word are adjacent, but not in order. Find them and rearrange them to spell a word. Cross out those letters and imagine that the six remaining letters are now consecutive. These remaining letters can now be rearranged to spell the second word.

Example: ALCUERHTLPEA. UERHTL can be rearranged into HURTLE. That leaves ALCPEA, which can be rearranged into PALACE.

NIHIVYOONCWT

OHHCIOULNNCO

OELTOCYRUAMR

IBACUIONSRFC

BANANA PUDDING

Each of the two-letter groups below may be extended both on the right and the left to form a six-letter word. Drawing from the tiles directly above each group, fill in the blanks to find the words as quickly as you can.

A E N O T T V

☐ ☐ N A ☐ ☐

D E I M O T V

☐ ☐ P E ☐ ☐

A B D N N R U

☐ ☐ H A ☐ ☐

A A C D F L P

☐ ☐ G O ☐ ☐

C E G N P R U

☐ ☐ B A ☐ ☐

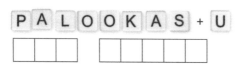

TOTALLY BANANAS

For each of the words below, replace one letter with the tile after the plus sign. Then rearrange the letters to form a city of the world.

P A L O O K A S + U

☐☐☐☐ ☐☐☐☐☐

R E G A L I A + S

☐☐☐☐☐☐☐

P A R E N T S + W

☐☐☐☐☐☐☐

S A W L O G S + G

☐☐☐☐☐☐☐

S P I L L O V E R + O

☐☐☐☐☐☐☐☐☐☐

C A V E R N O U S + V

☐☐☐☐☐☐☐☐☐

BANANA TREES

Use the 15 tiles in this bunch to create words that fit into the grids below. To get you started, a few tiles from the bunch have been placed in the grid. Reuse the 15 tiles in the bunch for each grid.

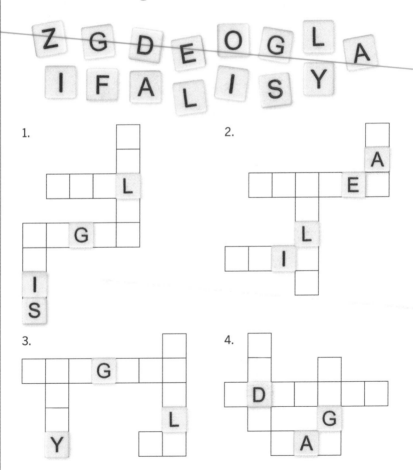

BUNCH OF BANANAS

For each word or phrase below, rearrange the letters to spell two things that can be white. For example, FOAMY SOLS can be rearranged to spell MAYO, FLOSS. The last letter of each word is placed to get you started.

AVENGE — PEOPLE

☐☐☐☐☐☐☐E ☐☐☐E

LOUD — CHEEPS

☐☐☐☐D ☐☐☐☐☐P

CALM — HACKER

☐☐☐☐K ☐☐☐☐☐M

THESPIAN — RITE

☐☐☐☐☐H ☐☐☐☐☐☐☐N

AGUE — ZAPPER

☐☐☐☐E ☐☐☐☐☐R

GOUGES — OARS

☐☐☐☐☐R ☐☐☐☐E

231

Rearrange the letters of each word below and place them in the blanks so that, together with the two letters that have already been placed, they form a new word.

P L O T S

A _ _ _ _ E

C H O L O

A _ _ _ _ _ L

M I N E S

A _ _ _ _ A

N O V E L

E _ _ _ _ P

BANANA FILLING

Add a T to each of the words below and then rearrange the letters in each word to form a new seven-letter word.

Using four of the tiles from the bunch on the left, fill in the blanks on the right to make a seven-letter word that connects the grid.

233

BANANA SHAKES

Each of the following six-letter sets can be rearranged to spell out a common word that either starts with C, D, or I _and/or_ ends with B, F, or P. Find all the words as quickly as you can.

E I N N T V

A B E F H L

A L O P P T

C E H L O T

B B C E O W

A C I N T T

B C E H R U

A D I M N O

A C C G N O

A F F L O Y

A G L L O P

D G O T U U

BANANA PEELS

There is <u>one letter</u> that when added to all of the five-letter words below can be used to form new six-letter words. Find the letter that works for all four words, add it to each word, and then rearrange each set of letters to form a new word. For example, L can be added to ROADS, WEARY, EPICS and GONER to form DORSAL, LAWYER, SPLICE and LONGER.

COMMON
LETTER

F L A Y S

L A T H E

R I V E T

S C O N E

BANANARAMA

Each of the words below can be turned into another word on the list by changing one letter and then rearranging them all to form a new word. For example, REGIMENT can be turned into STEERING by changing the M to an S, so they would be a pair. How quickly can you find all the pairs?

Pairs

1. WHATSIS ___ ___
2. MUSKRAT ___ ___
3. BECLOUD — —
4. THEREOF ___ ___
5. INBUILT — —
6. LOUDISH
7. LOCULED
8. ATRIUMS
9. PITSAWS
10. HEFTERS
11. UNSOLID
12. NAUTILI

Each set of letters below is arranged alphabetically, and the ? is in the correct alphabetical position. Figure out what letter the ? represents and rearrange the letters to spell a six-letter word. For example, in A?ENTV the ? could be an A, B, C, D or E. Here it represents a D, which can be combined with the other letters to spell ADVENT. The last letter is placed to get you started.

E E I O R ?

| | | | | | E |

A B G ? L O

| | | | | | L |

E P R S U ?

| | | | | | E |

A B H I O ?

| | | | | | A |

E M ? S U U

| | | | | | M |

? F I M N Y

| | | | | | Y |

A C L M ? U

| | | | | | M |

A A A R ? V

| | | | | | R |

A A D P ? Y

| | | | | | Y |

A A A E ? Z

| | | | | | A |

TOP BANANA

For each bunch below, rearrange the letters to form two intersecting words that fit into the corresponding grid.

BANANA CRUNCH

Each set of 12 tiles below contains two common six-letter words. The letters of the first six-letter word are adjacent, but not in order. Find them and rearrange them to spell a word. Cross out those letters and imagine that the six remaining letters are now consecutive. These remaining letters can now be rearranged to spell the second word.

Example: ALCUERHTLPEA. UERHTL can be rearranged into HURTLE. That leaves ALCPEA, which can be rearranged into PALACE.

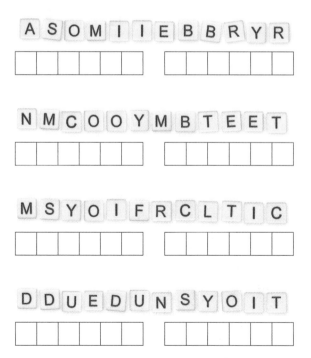

A S O M I I E B B R Y R

N M C O O Y M B T E E T

M S Y O I F R C L T I C

D D U E D U N S Y O I T

BANANA PUDDING

Each of the two-letter groups below may be extended both on the right and the left to form a six-letter word. Drawing from the tiles directly above each group, fill in the blanks to find the words as quickly as you can.

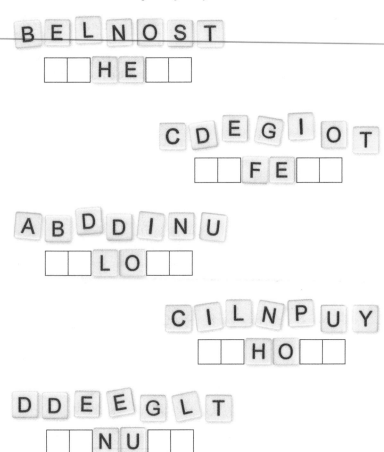

B E L N O S T
☐ ☐ H E ☐ ☐

C D E G I O T
☐ ☐ F E ☐ ☐

A B D D I N U
☐ ☐ L O ☐ ☐

C I L N P U Y
☐ ☐ H O ☐ ☐

D D E E G L T
☐ ☐ N U ☐ ☐

TOTALLY BANANAS

For each of the words below, replace one letter with the tile after the plus sign. Then rearrange the letters to form an adjective a critic might use.

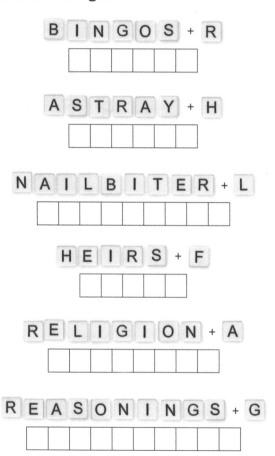

B I N G O S + R

⬜⬜⬜⬜⬜⬜

A S T R A Y + H

⬜⬜⬜⬜⬜⬜

N A I L B I T E R + L

⬜⬜⬜⬜⬜⬜⬜⬜⬜

H E I R S + F

⬜⬜⬜⬜⬜

R E L I G I O N + A

⬜⬜⬜⬜⬜⬜⬜⬜

R E A S O N I N G S + G

⬜⬜⬜⬜⬜⬜⬜⬜⬜⬜

BANANA TREES

Use the 15 tiles in this bunch to create words that fit into the grids below. To get you started, a few tiles from the bunch have been placed in the grid. Reuse the 15 tiles in the bunch for each grid.

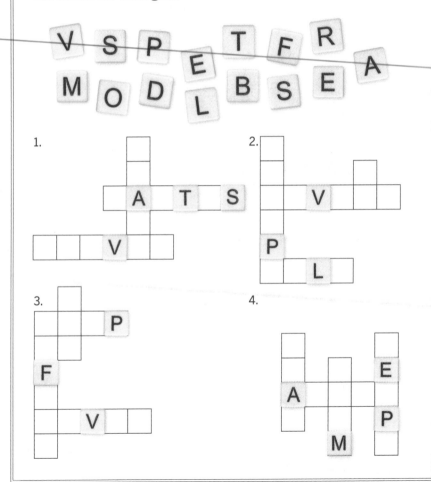

BUNCH OF BANANAS

For each word or phrase below, rearrange the letters to spell two new words that are each types of curved or circular objects. For example, BIGGER FEES can be rearranged to spell EGG, FRISBEE. The last letter of each word is placed to get you started.

I BLAME PLATE
☐☐☐☐☐☐☐ L ☐☐ E

RIPE PETAL
☐☐☐☐ E ☐☐☐☐ E

HALLOWEEN HEM
☐☐☐☐☐ L ☐☐☐☐☐☐☐ E

BATON TUMBLER
☐☐☐☐☐ N ☐☐☐☐☐☐ E

MOON SPUN RHYME
☐☐☐☐☐☐☐☐ M ☐☐☐☐☐ Y

ROWING BRAIN
☐☐☐☐☐☐☐ W ☐☐☐ G

Rearrange the letters of each word below and place them in the blanks so that, together with the two letters that have already been placed, they form a new word.

CARET

D _ _ _ _ T

PATIO

C _ _ _ _ L

PANIC

S _ _ _ _ H

SPENT

A _ _ _ _ S

BANANA FILLING

Add an N to each of the words below and then rearrange the letters in each word to form a new seven-letter word.

Using four of the tiles from the bunch on the left, fill in the blanks on the right to make a seven-letter word that connects the grid.

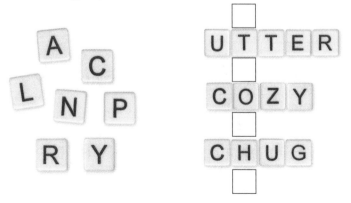

BANANA SHAKES

Each of the following six-letter sets can be rearranged to spell out a common word that either starts with R, S, or T <u>and/or</u> ends with N, R, or Y. Find all the words as quickly as you can.

A L N O O S

C E I O P R

B I N N O U

E I L M T Y

E E F R T U

A A N W Y Y

A A E G S V

A E O P T T

A I R R T Y

C E E L R V

B E I N T T

E G H H I R

BANANA PEELS

There is <u>one letter</u> that when added to all of the five-letter words below can be used to form new six-letter words. Find the letter that works for all four words, add it to each word, and then rearrange each set of letters to form a new word. For example, L can be added to ROADS, WEARY, EPICS and GONER to form DORSAL, LAWYER, SPLICE and LONGER.

COMMON
LETTER

[ ]

F A R C E

[ ][ ][ ][ ][ ][ ]

G R A V E

[ ][ ][ ][ ][ ][ ]

A M I N E

[ ][ ][ ][ ][ ][ ]

C O I F S

[ ][ ][ ][ ][ ][ ]

BANANARAMA

Each of the words below can be turned into another word on the list by changing one letter and then rearranging them all to form a new word. For example, REGIMENT can be turned into STEERING by changing the M to an S, so they would be a pair. How quickly can you find all the pairs?

Pairs

1. R O B O T I C   __ __
2. A N O M A L Y   __ __
3. H A B I T A N   __ __
4. L I V E N E D   __ __
5. S Y C O N I A   __ __
6. H O S T I L E   __ __
7. A B S T A I N
8. A C T I O N S
9. M A Y O R A L
10. P O R T I C O
11. B E D E V I L
12. C O L T I S H

BANANA CHIPS

Each set of letters below is arranged alphabetically, and the
? is in the correct alphabetical position. Figure out what
letter the ? represents and rearrange the letters to spell
a six-letter word. For example, in A?ENTV the ? could be
an A, B, C, D or E. Here it represents a D, which can be
combined with the other letters to spell ADVENT. The last
letter is placed to get you started.

C I I M T ?

| | | | | | M |

A C ? S T W

| | | | | | H |

D E E G ? N

| | | | | | D |

A E E K ? T

| | | | | | E |

B G H ? T U

| | | | | | T |

E ? L O U W

| | | | | | L |

C E E ? S W

| | | | | | W |

A E R R ? Y

| | | | | | Y |

B ? E I O X

| | | | | | X |

D ? O R U V

| | | | | | R |

For each bunch below, rearrange the letters to form two intersecting words that fit into the corresponding grid.

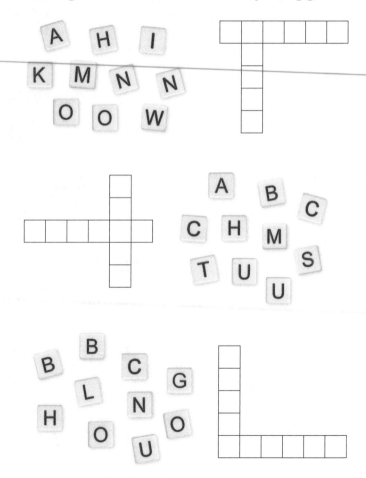

BANANA CRUNCH

Each set of 12 tiles below contains two common six-letter words. The letters of the first six-letter word are adjacent, but not in order. Find them and rearrange them to spell a word. Cross out those letters and imagine that the six remaining letters are now consecutive. These remaining letters can now be rearranged to spell the second word.

Example: **ALCUERHTLPEA. UERHTL** can be rearranged into **HURTLE.** That leaves **ALCPEA,** which can be rearranged into **PALACE.**

D S S A E E M U W I N N

L H U E D N N O A E E R

O R S A R S U Y G H U D

T E E N G T M A P C O I

BANANA PUDDING

Each of the two-letter groups below may be extended both on the right and the left to form a six-letter word. Drawing from the tiles directly above each group, fill in the blanks to find the words as quickly as you can.

TOTALLY BANANAS

For each of the words below, replace one letter with the
tile after the plus sign. Then rearrange the letters to form
a word related to mathematics.

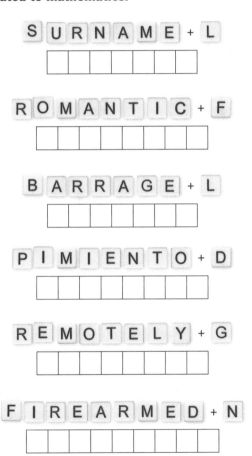

S U R N A M E + L

R O M A N T I C + F

B A R R A G E + L

P I M I E N T O + D

R E M O T E L Y + G

F I R E A R M E D + N

BANANA TREES

Use the 15 tiles in this bunch to create words that fit into the grids below. To get you started, a few tiles from the bunch have been placed in the grid. Reuse the 15 tiles in the bunch for each grid.

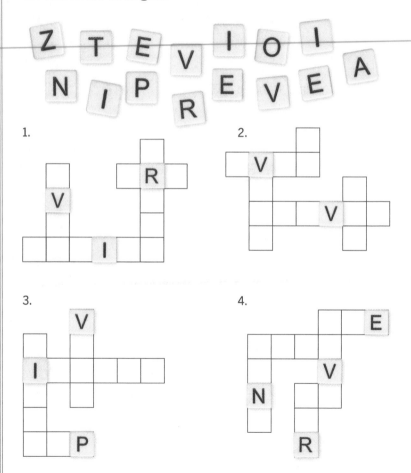

BUNCH OF BANANAS

For each word or phrase below, rearrange the letters to spell two things that can be sharp. For example, SENTINEL COP can be rearranged to spell NOTES, PENCIL. The last letter of each word is placed to get you started.

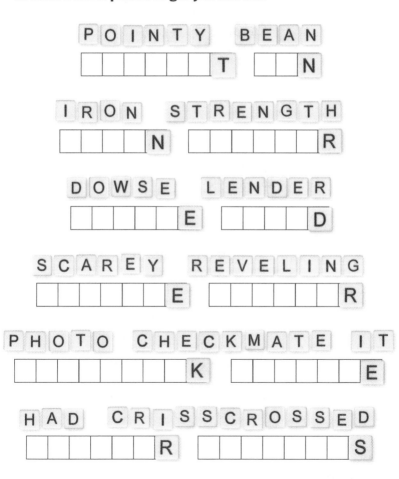

POINTY   BEAN

| | | | | | | T | | | N |

IRON   STRENGTH

| | | | | N | | | | | | | | R |

DOWSE   LENDER

| | | | | | E | | | | | D |

SCAREY   REVELING

| | | | | | | E | | | | | | | R |

PHOTO   CHECKMATE   IT

| | | | | | | | | K | | | | | | | | E |

HAD   CRISSCROSSED

| | | | | | R | | | | | | | | | S |

Rearrange the letters of each word below and place them in the blanks so that, together with the two letters that have already been placed, they form a new word.

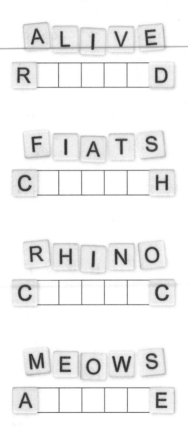

ALIVE

R _ _ _ _ D

FIATS

C _ _ _ _ H

RHINO

C _ _ _ _ C

MEOWS

A _ _ _ _ E

BANANA FILLING

Add a K **to each of the words below and then rearrange the letters in each word to form a new seven-letter word.**

G L O W E R

B I T E R S

P E A R L S

D U N C E S

Using four of the tiles from the bunch on the left, fill in the blanks on the right to make a seven-letter word that connects the grid.

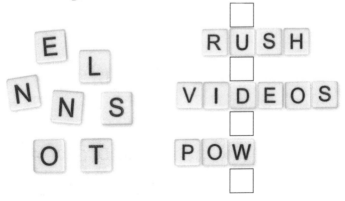

E
N L
N S
O T

R U S H
V I D E O S
P O W

BANANA SHAKES

Each of the following six-letter sets can be rearranged to spell out a common word that either starts with C, F, or P **and/or** ends with G, H, or M. Find all the words as quickly as you can.

E G G G N O

A F H M O T

A L M S U Y

A C E E L V

B E G L N O

A B H I N S

G H O R T W

A A C C D I

B M O O T T

A C F I P Y

A F L T U Y

A A D G O P

BANANA PEELS

There is <u>one letter</u> that when added to all of the five-letter words below can be used to form new six-letter words. Find the letter that works for all four words, add it to each word, and then rearrange each set of letters to form a new word. For example, L can be added to ROADS, WEARY, EPICS and GONER to form DORSAL, LAWYER, SPLICE and LONGER.

COMMON
LETTER

T U N I C

C H E A T

A F O R E

W H E A T

BANANARAMA

Each of the words below can be turned into another word on the list by changing one letter and then rearranging them all to form a new word. For example, REGIMENT can be turned into STEERING by changing the M to an S, so they would be a pair. How quickly can you find all the pairs?

1. O N E S E L F

2. A M P O U L E

3. M I N U T I A

4. A I R H E A D

5. A N A L Y S T

6. M A N U M I T

7. L E U C O M A

8. H A L O G E N

9. E N C L O S E

10. R A W H I D E

11. S E A L A N T

12. A G E L O N G

Pairs

—— ——

—— ——

—— ——

—— ——

—— ——

—— ——

260

BANANA CHIPS

Each set of letters below is arranged alphabetically, and the
? is in the correct alphabetical position. Figure out what
letter the ? represents and rearrange the letters to spell
a six-letter word. For example, in A?ENTV the ? could be
an A, B, C, D or E. Here it represents a D, which can be
combined with the other letters to spell ADVENT. The last
letter is placed to get you started.

A A G ? R U
[ ] [ ] [ ] [ ] [ ] R

D E I ? M W
[ ] [ ] [ ] [ ] [ ] W

E E E L N ?
[ ] [ ] [ ] [ ] [ ] N

D E E ? M P
[ ] [ ] [ ] [ ] [ ] E

D F I ? O R
[ ] [ ] [ ] [ ] [ ] D

D E ? P U X
[ ] [ ] [ ] [ ] [ ] X

E G L O ? Y
[ ] [ ] [ ] [ ] [ ] Y

A I O P T ?
[ ] [ ] [ ] [ ] [ ] A

B I M ? T U
[ ] [ ] [ ] [ ] [ ] T

E F F G ? Y
[ ] [ ] [ ] [ ] [ ] Y

TOP BANANA

For each bunch below, rearrange the letters to form two intersecting words that fit into the corresponding grid.

BANANA CRUNCH

Each set of 12 tiles below contains two common six-letter words. The letters of the first six-letter word are adjacent, but not in order. Find them and rearrange them to spell a word. Cross out those letters and imagine that the six remaining letters are now consecutive. These remaining letters can now be rearranged to spell the second word.

Example: **ALCUERHTLPEA. UERHTL** can be rearranged into **HURTLE.** That leaves **ALCPEA,** which can be rearranged into **PALACE.**

R A H E E O M N G T X O

[ ][ ][ ][ ][ ][ ]   [ ][ ][ ][ ][ ][ ]

G H G U A P N R L U V A

[ ][ ][ ][ ][ ][ ]   [ ][ ][ ][ ][ ][ ]

H T G A E O Y V M A W R

[ ][ ][ ][ ][ ][ ]   [ ][ ][ ][ ][ ][ ]

L M A E Y C L G N O A R

[ ][ ][ ][ ][ ][ ]   [ ][ ][ ][ ][ ][ ]

BANANA PUDDING

Each of the two-letter groups below may be extended both on the right and the left to form a six-letter word. Drawing from the tiles directly above each group, fill in the blanks to find the words as quickly as you can.

A E G M P R T

☐ ☐ N U ☐ ☐

A E F K O R T

☐ ☐ N A ☐ ☐

A D I L N R T

☐ ☐ M O ☐ ☐

B E F I L M O

☐ ☐ P A ☐ ☐

A C D F L S U

☐ ☐ M O ☐ ☐

TOTALLY BANANAS

For each of the words below, replace one letter with the tile after the plus sign. Then rearrange the letters to form a popular card game.

S E C U R E + H

M U R K Y + M

B I R D C A G E + B

A E R I A L I S T + O

C A T A R A C T + B

C A T N A P S + A

BANANA TREES

Use the 15 tiles in this bunch to create words that fit into the grids below. To get you started, a few tiles from the bunch have been placed in the grid. Reuse the 15 tiles in the bunch for each grid.

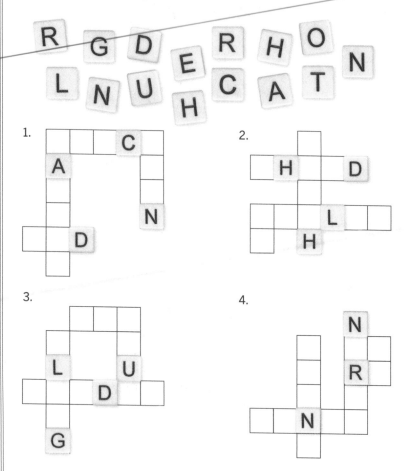

BUNCH OF BANANAS

For each word or phrase below, rearrange the letters to spell two new words that are homonyms. For example, AGE WITH WIT can be rearranged to spell WAIT, WEIGHT. The last letter of each word is placed to get you started.

R O L L   K E E N   C L O N E

☐☐☐☐☐☐ L   ☐☐☐☐☐ L

T R A C K   A   T E A R

☐☐☐☐ T   ☐☐☐☐ T

S E E D   H I S   D I G

☐☐☐ E   ☐☐☐☐☐ D

S A W   R E D   D O O R S

☐☐☐☐☐ D   ☐☐☐☐ D

D E W Y   S E A S   D U E

☐☐☐☐ E   ☐☐☐☐☐ D

C U T   H O T   S H O E

☐☐☐☐ E   ☐☐☐☐ T

267

Rearrange the letters of each word below and place them in the blanks so that, together with the two letters that have already been placed, they form a new word.

BAITS

A _ _ _ _ N

GRACE

A _ _ _ _ E

TRUES

G _ _ _ _ E

RAVEL

O _ _ _ _ P

BANANA FILLING

Add an L to each of the words below and then rearrange the letters in each word to form a new seven-letter word.

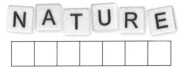

Using four of the tiles from the bunch on the left, fill in the blanks on the right to make a seven-letter word that connects the grid.

BANANA SHAKES

Each of the following six-letter sets can be rearranged to spell out a common word that either starts with L , M , or O and/or ends with E , L , or R . Find all the words as quickly as you can.

A B F G L U

B D E O R T

C E E N O R

A E L M R V

A L L S T Y

E O O P P S

E F F K O Y

A L N R X Y

C E I K O O

A A C F I L

E H K N R U

E E M M N R

BANANA PEELS

There is <u>one letter</u> that when added to all of the five-letter words below can be used to form new six-letter words. Find the letter that works for all four words, add it to each word, and then rearrange each set of letters to form a new word. For example, L can be added to ROADS, WEARY, EPICS and GONER to form DORSAL, LAWYER, SPLICE and LONGER.

COMMON
LETTER

[ ]

L E G A L

[ ] [ ] [ ] [ ] [ ] [ ]

R E M A P

[ ] [ ] [ ] [ ] [ ] [ ]

H A M M Y

[ ] [ ] [ ] [ ] [ ] [ ]

C O A L S

[ ] [ ] [ ] [ ] [ ] [ ]

BANANARAMA

Each of the words below can be turned into another word on the list by changing one letter and then rearranging them all to form a new word. For example, REGIMENT can be turned into STEERING by changing the M to an S, so they would be a pair. How quickly can you find all the pairs?

Pairs

1. A D R E N A L

___ ___

2. A L L E G R O

___ ___

3. U R E T H R A

___ ___

4. U N B R A C E

___ ___

5. M A N A C L E

___ ___

6. A I R F O I L

7. C U R A B L E

8. B A L A N C E

9. L O Y A L E R

10. R A V I O L I

11. R A P T U R E

12. G A R L A N D

BANANA CHIPS

Each set of letters below is arranged alphabetically, and the **?** is in the correct alphabetical position. Figure out what letter the **?** represents and rearrange the letters to spell a six-letter word. For example, in A?ENTV the **?** could be an A, B, C, D or E. Here it represents a D, which can be combined with the other letters to spell ADVENT. The last letter is placed to get you started.

E F N O ? T
| | | | | | N |

B ? E M O Y
| | | | | | Y |

A C E ? H U
| | | | | | E |

A L O ? U W
| | | | | | W |

E E O ? T Y
| | | | | | E |

E F ? L N U
| | | | | | F |

E I I L ? U
| | | | | | U |

B ? O P U W
| | | | | | P |

D G I I ? O
| | | | | | O |

E E ? I L N
| | | | | | E |

273

ANSWER KEY

PAGE 14
ARMPIT, PREACH, CARPET, ENDEAR

PAGE 15
PASTRY, CLASSY, STRESS, TYPIST

NAPKIN

PAGE 16
CUTEST, REBORN, PARLOR, BLITHE, GLAMOR, REDUCE, ROBUST, BESTOW, ENGINE, YELLOW, ENMITY, BLOWUP

PAGE 17
M: IMPEL, PRIME, LEMUR, MIDST

PAGE 18
1–5, 2–8, 3–11, 4–9, 6–12, 7–10

PAGE 19
WEEKLY, SUFFIX, WITHIN, ALWAYS, PIGLET, LEGUME, CHERUB, WALNUT, MELODY, BECOME

PAGE 20

PAGE 21
AGENT/ADAPT; VITAL/BRAND; GUAVA/APART; CRAZY/BATHE

PAGE 22
RAINED, BRUTAL, RAISIN, POINTY, POODLE

PAGE 23
PEDALS, AIRBAG, ENGINE, RADIO, ODOMETER, SEATBELT

PAGE 24

PAGE 25
OLIVES, LAWN; APPLE, TREES; MONEY, SAGE; CELERY, PEAS; MOLD, ELVES; SPINACH, KELP

PAGE 26
HEREBY, DISARM, GARDEN, DANCER

PAGE 27
CURLER, HARBOR, PARLOR, STURDY

IMPAIR

PAGE 28
GLITCH, BECOME, FLUENT, GENTLE, CAVING, LEGUME, FOIBLE, WIPING, CLOSET, CLAUSE, GLANCE, FLORAL

PAGE 29
G: GLOAT, RUGBY, COUGH, URGED

PAGE 30
1–8, 2–9, 3–12, 4–7, 5–10, 6–11

PAGE 31
CHATTY, FRUGAL, AFFORD, FRIGID, GAUGED, MODULE, BIRDIE, HUMBUG, WIZARD, COLUMN

PAGE 32

PAGE 33
COLOR/LYRIC; NOTCH/HANDY; DWELL/WEDGE; LOGIC/MUNCH

PAGE 34
AMOEBA, BEATEN, OVERDO, HIATUS, HOOPLA

PAGE 35
MELODY, LYRICS, BEAT, TEMPO, CHORUS, VERSE

PAGE 36

1.

2.

3.

4.

PAGE 37
CHEF, WAITER; TEACHER, PUPIL; WRITER, ACTOR; DOCTOR, NURSE; AUTHOR, EDITOR; RABBI, CANTOR

PAGE 38
PERSON, ASLEEP, LOCALE, SEARCH

PAGE 39
AROUND, UTOPIA, RITUAL, MEDIUM

INDUCT

PAGE 40
ABACUS, CANYON, BUSILY, DEBATE, ARCHER, INCITE, DECODE, INFUSE, COMPLY, BOTHER, DRAGON, ABDUCT

PAGE 41
Y: ROYAL, YEAST, SPACY, FIFTY

PAGE 42
1–12, 2–7, 3–10, 4–9, 5–8, 6–11

PAGE 43
FORAGE, OXFORD, BEYOND, TUXEDO, PUBLIC, UNUSED, DOLLOP, SCHISM, REVERE, COFFEE

PAGE 44

PAGE 45
SLASH/BOTCH; TRAIT/BLUNT; KABOB/TENTH; PECAN/PLACE

PAGE 46
PROMPT, WOODEN, TOUPEE, OPENLY, ENAMEL

PAGE 47
POKER, CASINO, HEARTS, BRIDGE, RUMMY, SPADES

PAGE 48
1.

2.

3.

4.

PAGE 49
AWFUL, OFFAL; ALLOWED, ALOUD; PACKED, PACT; PAUSE, PAWS; REIGN, RAIN; TIGHTEN, TITAN

PAGE 50
CENSOR, RUSTIC, CUSTOM, RETURN

PAGE 51
ABSENT, HAMLET, ATTEST, GIBLET

UNMASK

PAGE 52
BIGWIG, COLLAR, AMORAL, BUNGEE, DEGREE, BIONIC, THWART, CLIENT, COBALT, INVERT, AMOUNT, FLAUNT

PAGE 53
F: SCARF, DWARF, FEWER, FRESH

PAGE 54
1–7, 2–5, 3–9, 4–12, 6–10, 8–11

PAGE 55
PUSHUP, VANISH, JERSEY, WALLOP, DRAFTY, PEANUT, PEWTER, PAJAMA, PAYOFF, MUTANT

PAGE 56

PAGE 57
LEGAL/FAINT; STASH/VERGE; RIGOR/JUNKY; FUROR/TEPID

PAGE 58
LAPELS, GOATEE, SIERRA, MYOPIC, PLANET

PAGE 59
HAZY, ROUND, DARK, BRIGHT, ORANGE, MATCHING

PAGE 60
1.

2.

3.

4.

PAGE 61
ASLEEP, AWAKE; RIGHT, LEFT; STRONG, WEAK; ONE, MANY; ENTER, EXIT; BIG, LITTLE

PAGE 62
UNWRAP, TOMATO, MUTANT, WEIRDO

PAGE 63
WEAPON, SWEATY, WEALTH, CASHEW

DUGOUT

PAGE 64
CREAMY, COCOON, NEATEN, MUFFIN, SCRIPT, COLLIE, MADMAN, SCENIC, ATTAIN, CRISIS, DEMEAN, ACUMEN

PAGE 65
H: DUTCH, ETHIC, HEDGE, BUSHY

PAGE 66
1–7, 2–11, 3–12, 4–10, 5–9, 6–8

PAGE 67
EXEMPT, HELMET, NEPHEW, EYEFUL, BOUNCE, OBEYED, OXYGEN, CIRCUS, PELLET, HYPHEN

PAGE 68

```
FEWER
O
L
I
O
          P
      RIGOR
          L
          O
          T
VINYL
    O
    U
    T
    H
```

PAGE 69
EXCEL/MODEL; DONUT/FLEET; FOYER/MOTIF; PUPIL/HOLLY

PAGE 70
SEAMAN, ACUMEN, COUNTY, PROFIT, CHOSEN

PAGE 71
RAKE, KNIFE, WRENCH, DRILL, HAMMER, PLIERS

PAGE 72

1.
```
          N
A         E
L         A
I         R
BOOTIES
I
```
2.
```
          I
          O
  R       T
  I     BOA
ALIENS
  E
```

3.
```
    BE
    I
ORATION
    E
    SAIL
```
4.
```
AISLE
  O
  I
OBTAIN
  E
  R
```

PAGE 73
PEN, BLADE; WIT, SPIKE; CLAW, DAGGER; FORK, CACTUS; TACK, SABER; FANG, KNIFE

PAGE 74
BRONCO, DREAMY, HERMIT, CARROT

PAGE 75
NOVICE, WEIRDO, TEDIUM, MISUSE, BANDIT

PAGE 76
FRUGAL, DEDUCT, INHALE, UPWARD, FRIGID, UNWIND, ONWARD, INDOOR, PLEDGE, INDICT, GROUND, PLOUGH

PAGE 77
V: RAVEN, VITAL, UVULA, HEAVY

PAGE 78
1–9, 2–7, 3–10, 4–12, 5–8, 6–11

PAGE 79
PIGPEN, CRISIS, UNWISE, HELIUM, ENOUGH, ZENITH, HOGTIE, TIDBIT, FERVOR, ZEPHYR

PAGE 80

```
        M
        A
        M
        B
GUMBO   O
CLOAK
    L
    U
    T
    Z
    R
CIGAR
    I
    D
```

PAGE 81
CROWD/MULCH; BLOOD/ANNEX; LADLE/DECAY; FRAUD/VALET

PAGE 82
UNISON, EGOISM, TENURE, STEREO, IGNORE

PAGE 83
SQUARE, SPHERE, CIRCLE, HEART, DIAMOND, ELLIPSE

PAGE 84

1.
```
      B
G     R
O     O
O     K
PIXIES
      I
      T
```
2.
```
  PIT
    I
    C
    K
BOXERS
O     I
GOGO
```

3.
```
BOOKIE
I     X
G     I
      S
   PORT
```
4.
```
    B
    I
  TOG R
O   I I
K   EXPOS
```

PAGE 85
BASE, CORN; FOOT, BEAN; FIRE, MEAT; GOOF, FAST; SPIT, HAIR; BEACH, PIN

PAGE 86
NEARBY, MIDWAY, ZENITH, FORGET

PAGE 87
OCTANE, ROADIE, ADROIT, BARRIO

AUTHOR

PAGE 88
ETHNIC, FLINCH, MELODY, UNPACK, PELVIS, FROLIC, ATTACK, DECEIT,

GROUCH, PENCIL,
MEMOIR, DEFLEA

PAGE 89
B: BYLAW, EMBED,
BONGO, BISON

PAGE 90
1–12, 2–8, 3–7,
4–9, 5–11, 6–10

PAGE 91
KENNEL, INFECT,
ENZYME, OVERDO,
AVENUE, LAWYER,
UPSIDE, FUNNEL,
STYMIE, PACKET

PAGE 92

PAGE 93
JOINT/BANAL;
WRING/VIGIL;
TWEAK/HOUSE;
KHAKI/KAZOO

PAGE 94
MEASLY, PRONTO,
PLAGUE, ENERGY,
VOYAGE

PAGE 95
ANGLE or ALIGN,
GRAPH, PRIME,
DIGIT, RADIUS,
FACTOR

PAGE 96

1.

2.

3.

4.

PAGE 97
MILK, RICE;
IVORY, SOAP;
SALT, BREAD;
NOISE, TUB;
SNOW, IGLOO;
LIGHT, SAND

PAGE 98
NUTMEG,
GOSPEL, BISECT,
SALMON

PAGE 99
CHORAL, HARDLY,
LAVISH, SULTAN

UPLOAD

PAGE 100
WRENCH, REVOLT,
NONFAT, THRASH,
UNSEAT, SEESAW,
THEORY, OUTLAW,

EMBRYO, TUMULT,
WRYEST, EMPLOY

PAGE 101
E: AFTER, METAL,
WEIGH, OBOES

PAGE 102
1–10, 2–4, 3–7,
5–11, 6–8, 9–12

PAGE 103
FATHOM, GLADLY,
MOHAIR, BISHOP,
SHOULD, BESTOW,
PICKUP, PARDON,
TYCOON, FLAVOR

PAGE 104

PAGE 105
KIOSK/MINOR;
LYMPH/WHEAT;
DOUBT/DATED;
PANDA/MADAM

PAGE 106
TWELVE, PLASMA,
POORLY, STUPID,
REOPEN

PAGE 107
RISK, CHESS,
SORRY,
STRATEGO,
OTHELLO,
CHECKERS

PAGE 108

1.

2.

3.

4.

PAGE 109

LARGE, BIG;
RED, SCARLET;
BLUE, SAD;
ARMS, WEAPONS;
COUNT, TALLY;
COVER, SHELTER

PAGE 110
ENGAGE, TAWDRY,
CLOSET, IMPURE

PAGE 111
SKYCAP, ASYLUM,
SWAYED, CRAYON

SIPHON

PAGE 112
LAWMEN,
PROPER, BIOPIC,
ANYHOW,
ECHOED, MALADY,
PRINCE, ANGLER,
BROKEN, IRONIC,
MADCAP, IMBUED

PAGE 113
C: WHACK, FETCH, COUNT, CHUMS

PAGE 114
1–11, 2–10, 3–7, 4–9, 5–8, 6–12

PAGE 115
GALLON, ZODIAC, TOMATO, FAUCET, WALRUS, BEHIND, ZEALOT, WARMTH, HEAVEN, MATRIX

PAGE 116

FAULT
N
D
I
D

U
N
C
U
NINTH

PRIVY
H
O
T
O

PAGE 117
VIGOR/NANNY;
ALOHA/WAFER;
GAUZE/INANE;
PRICE/FOUND

PAGE 118
MAIDEN, BIOPSY, TROWEL, FLORID, AVOWAL

PAGE 119
FROG, FALCON, COYOTE, LEOPARD, HYENA, PANDA

PAGE 120
1.

D
HAZE E
VAT T
T E
FED R

2.
H
DAZED
V
FEET
TAR
T

3.
FED
V
T E
HAZARD
T T
E

4.
A
V
DATED R F
R TEETH
Z

PAGE 121
ARC, PEA;
CIRCLE, DOT;
NUT, SPHERE;
EYE, ORBIT;
BULB, BAGEL;
PLANET, SUN

PAGE 122
ORDAIN, ENROBE, BRAWNY, POLICE

PAGE 123
BASKET, KISMET, SPOKEN, SKETCH

CASUAL

PAGE 124
AWHILE, DREDGE, AERIAL, PEOPLE, ADVENT, ORPHAN, TROPHY, TRAUMA, ADRIFT, ANNUAL, DROWSY, BEDPAN

PAGE 125
P: PADDY, ADOPT, SHIPS, BLIMP

PAGE 126
1–9, 2–6, 3–12, 4–8, 5–11, 7–10

PAGE 127
ELICIT, TOFFEE, BOUNCY, PODIUM, OBLONG, TAUGHT, CAVITY, VOLUME, BUTTON, LAYMAN

PAGE 128

M
O
G
OCCUR
L

M
E
R
PIECE
Y

PANDA
L
O
U
D

PAGE 129
HENNA/HALVE;
WEAVE/DRAWL;
TRACT/BLIMP;
NIECE/CLEFT

PAGE 130
WHITEN, ENABLE, NUANCE, COUPON, BUOYED

PAGE 131
BROMINE, ARGON, CALCIUM, SILICON, MAGNESIUM, CHROMIUM

PAGE 132

1.

G C
VINEGAR E
M E
TEE P

2.
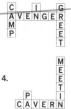
G
CREATING
E V M
E E P

3.
C I G
AVENGER R
M E E
P E T

4.
M
E
E
T
P I
CAVERN G
G E
E

PAGE 133
UPSET, SAFE;
WEARY, PROUD;
GLAD, SCARED;
SECURE, LOVED;
EAGER, SORRY;
MAD, RELAXED

PAGE 134
CAMERA, UMLAUT, MARINA, SNIVEL

PAGE 135
SANDAL, VISAGE, SOAPED, ROTATE

NAUSEA

PAGE 136
ACIDIC, THEORY, BANANA, CHEESE, SONATA, THIRST, MYOPIA, ACTUAL, CABANA, HERNIA, ERRATA, CHIMED

PAGE 137
A: ALIAS, WAGER, TAKEN, AUGUR

PAGE 138
1–10, 2–8, 3–9, 4–7, 5–12, 6–11

PAGE 139
OCCULT, UNWRAP, AUGUST, FORMAT, PLAGUE, ANYHOW, HEREBY, CANDID, SUBPAR, FORBID

PAGE 140

PAGE 141
CHORD/FRAME; CUBIC/PANSY; AUGUR/ANNUL; FLAIL/WEARY

PAGE 142
SEANCE, MOTION, DEARTH, ADAGIO, THAWED

PAGE 143
CRAYONS, TOASTER, SLINKY, VELCRO, ZIPPER, RADAR

PAGE 144

1.
```
      C
    C O N S
      N
      V
      E X
I N J U R Y
```

2.
```
      C
    S O N
      R N
      V   Y
  J U I C Y
      X
      E
      N
```

3.
```
          C
J U N I O R S
      N   Y
      V   N
      E   C
      X
```

4.
```
S I X
  C
  O N J U R E
  N       N
          V
          Y
```

PAGE 145
TRIBE (baboons), BED (oysters); PRIDE (lions), DEN (snakes); NEST (hornets), PACK (bears); ARMY (ants), POD (dolphins); BEVY (quail), TEAM (cattle); PARADE (elephants), GAGGLE (geese)

PAGE 146
COMELY, PARODY, DYNAMO, UPLOAD

PAGE 147
DEMEAN, ANKLET, TAVERN, INFANT

VOYAGE

PAGE 148
PEANUT, SPIGOT, DEVOUR, WALNUT, HARASS, SPASMS, DICTUM, FOLKSY, POSSUM, CONCUR, HATPIN, FOURTH

PAGE 149
D: DEITY, FADED, VALID, SANDY

PAGE 150
1–8, 2–10, 3–6, 4–9, 5–11, 7–12

PAGE 151
REMEDY, IMPROV, BYLINE, EXHALE, PUEBLO, GULLET, MARVEL, FEWEST, FOODIE, CYBORG

PAGE 152

```
  B
A W A R E
Y
O
U
        O
        R
        B
        I
A B B O T
        A
Y A C H T
        A
        B
        O
        O
```

PAGE 153
ABACK/GUILD; GENIE/DITTO; CANAL/PEEVE; LAUGH/HELLO

PAGE 154
MEANIE, FELINE, STATUE, PRUNED, LOUNGE

PAGE 155
YODA, ALICE, BATMAN, KIRK, KERMIT, GANDALF

PAGE 156

1.
```
      J
  Q U I E T
      N
      G
      L
  S E R U M
      O
```

2.
```
        O M E N
            U
          J R
  Q U I L T S
          G E
```

3.
```
  J         M
  E         U
Q U E S T I O N
  R         G
            U
            L
```

4.
```
          J
          O
          L
      R G T
  Q U E U E S
      I M
      N
```

PAGE 157
CLOONEY, PITT ("Ocean's 11"); GERE, ROBERTS ("Pretty Woman"); DOUGLAS, CLOSE ("Fatal Attraction"); ASTAIRE, ROGERS ("The Gay Divorcee"); CRUISE, MOORE ("A Few Good Men"); BALE, LEDGER ("The Dark Knight")

PAGE 160
LOTTERY, LETDOWN, NOTABLE, SPONSOR

PAGE 161
ABILITY, DIETARY, EAGERLY, ANYMORE

MANMADE

PAGE 162
BALLAD, ENIGMA, BANKER, BASKET, DAHLIA, GALLEY, DEFECT, GADFLY, AGENDA, DECADE, BAMBOO, ANSWER

PAGE 163
P: PRANCE, TEACUP, CATNIP, SPOKEN

PAGE 164
1–7, 2–9, 3–12, 4–10, 5–8, 6–11

PAGE 165
INWARD, REVIVE, NOBODY, THEORY, COFFIN, HORRID, MAGNUM, TATTOO, STUDIO, BEFORE

PAGE 166

PAGE 167
SUBURB/BEHELD; PEPTIC/GOBLET; EITHER/SURFER;

INTENT/UNMASK

PAGE 168
UPLOAD, COBALT, BELONG, UNFAIR, PALACE

PAGE 169
MALLARD, TORTOISE, CHIMPANZEE, STURGEON, PEACOCK, CHAMELEON

PAGE 170
1.

2.

3.

4.

PAGE 171
HOME, DWELLING; AFRAID, SCARED; WARMTH, HEAT; SPORT, WEAR; GROW, DEVELOP; FLEET, FAST

PAGE 172
PATRIOT, OBESITY, EARLOBE, HAIRCUT

PAGE 173
SINCERE, PERSONA, DRAPERY, FIREMAN

UNLEASH

PAGE 174
GAMBIT, MOMENT, SCREWY, MEOWED, EMBARK, BEAUTY, MOCKUP, LEGACY, HELIUM, MUSEUM, SNITCH, ENCODE

PAGE 175
M: MUSSEL, MISHAP, CLAMOR, MADMEN

PAGE 176
1–5, 2–4, 3–10, 6–9, 7–11, 8–12

PAGE 177
HOTDOG, AUTUMN, DONKEY, MARKUP, PLURAL, PUTRID, REBOOT, FINITE, HERESY, JIGSAW

PAGE 178

PAGE 179
VISAGE/FACTOR; UNEASY/MARKET; FEMALE/COLUMN; HOORAH/MORTAL

PAGE 180
EULOGY, BEGONE, UPHELD, FINALE, LUNACY

PAGE 181
TRIANGLE, CRESCENT, RECTANGLE, TRAPEZOID, PENTAGRAM, RHOMBUS

PAGE 182
1.

2.

3.

4.

AVOCADO, LIME;
MOSS, LEAVES;
CUCUMBER,
HOLLY; GRASS
LETTUCE; JADE,
EMERALD;
ALLIGATOR, FERN

INCISOR,
SERPENT,
AIRPORT,
BENEATH

MISDRAW,
RAWHIDE,
EYEBROW,
BROWNIE

ABOLISH

MANTRA, PANTRY,
COLUMN, RAMROD,
FEWEST, PERMIT,
CRAYON, GENDER,
RADIUS, NAUSEA,
GENIUS, DIGEST

G: FLIGHT, PIGSTY,
TWANGS, SIGHED

1–10, 2–11, 3–7,
4–8, 5–9, 6–12

ELIXIR, EMBLEM,
WISDOM, BAKERY,
RENEGE, CONCUR,
DEPUTY, EXODUS,
GOALIE, DOLLAR

WALLET/FIGURE;
BALLET/HIJACK;
AUTUMN/AFFECT;
LEAGUE/PRANCE

UNHOOK, REDEEM,
RENOWN, PAPAYA,
INDOOR

DIPLOMACY,
CRANIUM,
PICTIONARY,
MASTERMIND,
BATTLESHIP,
MONOPOLY

1.

2.

3.

4.

DODGE, PAINT;
BLACK, EYE;
HARD, BUTTER;
SLIME, BASKET;
VOLLEY, CURVE;
EIGHT, HAND

EAGERLY,
AUDIBLE,
OREGANO,
PREDICT

BUOYANT,
MUSICAL,
CALLOUS,
CURATOR

ACRONYM

ICEBOX, FLEECE,
MILDEW, SLEIGH,
AMBUSH, EITHER,
POLISH, ELICIT,
ANYONE, ARRIVE,
IMMUNE, FELLOW

B: ABDUCT,
ABSORB, BEHAVE,
BYPASS

1–8, 2–7, 3–11, 4–9,
5–10, 6–12

PICNIC, PURITY,
HOOVES, PHOBIC,
DEPICT, COBALT,
CAVIAR, BUOYED,
UNFAIR, GAZEBO

ARMORY/PLURAL;
OBEYED/DEPICT;
PURSUE/
METHOD;
VISION/INJURY

OBLONG, DEFEND,
LAGOON, NEWEST,
UTMOST

PLANET, COMET,
ASTEROID,
SUPERNOVA,
SATELLITE,
QUASAR

1.

2.

3.

PARADE / RUDE / STARVED

4.

RUDDER / ADAPT / VERSE

PAGE 207
BUILD, DESTROY;
NEXT, PREVIOUS;
TRUE, FALSE; ADD,
REMOVE; LISTEN,
TALK; LEADER,
FOLLOWER

PAGE 208
GARMENT,
GENUINE,
NETWORK,
MONTAGE

PAGE 209
DISPELS, PASSION,
RESUMED,
GUESSED

MEASURE

PAGE 210
MIMOSA, METRIC,
HEAVEN, ASTRAY,
WARMTH,
MORASS, COUPON,
AROUND, EXOTIC,
MALLET, STIGMA,
WEIRDO

PAGE 211
V: RAVISH, VAINLY,
VICTOR, SVELTE

PAGE 212
1–9, 2–8, 3–7,
4–12, 5–11, 6–10

PAGE 213
REFUGE, WILDLY,

GOTHIC, CUCKOO,
DOMINO, UNDULY,
WEEVIL, VAINLY,
GENOME, BELFRY

PAGE 214

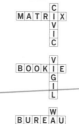

MATRIX / CVVIC

BOOKIE / VIGIL

BUREAU / WTCH

PAGE 215
HAIRDO/WEALTH;
HANDLE/POLICY;
COWBOY/TATTER;
ALBINO/BOYISH

PAGE 216
REDOES, ADMIRE,
MANUAL, TYPIST,
INLAID

PAGE 217
PAINTER,
CARTOONIST,
ILLUSTRATOR,
DESIGNER,
SCULPTOR,
ARCHITECT

PAGE 218
1.

RIOT / IRE / NUBKEWE

2.

RU / IU / REBUKE / O / TWINE

3.

BURRO / WIENIE / ETK

4.

ROT / KIOTURE / INURE / WEBE

PAGE 219
SPEAKER, AGENT;
PLAYER, COACH;
PRIEST, BISHOP;
FIREMAN, COP;
DANCER, SINGER;
ACTOR, DIRECTOR

PAGE 220
PLYWOOD,
WRANGLE,
WARSHIP,
SOLVENT

PAGE 221
PARAGON,
PARTIAL,
CAPTURE,
PAPERED

VARIETY

PAGE 222
PUMMEL,
TEMPER, CALICO,
TICKET, BANDIT,
GROVEL, FENNEL,
BOLERO, PRIMAL,
DITHER, FERVOR,
BEFORE

PAGE 223
C: CAVIAR,
CYMBAL, CREASE,
TACKLE

PAGE 224
1–6, 2–7, 3–9,
4–10, 5–11, 8–12

PAGE 225
BEAUTY, SAFELY,
IGUANA, SUNDRY,
THROAT, HUNGRY,
LIQUID, FUNGUS,
ENGAGE, ENGINE

PAGE 226

ABRUPT / BUILD / AVATAR / CRUMB / WIZARD / KARAT

PAGE 227
CONVOY/WITHIN;
UNCOIL/HONCHO;
OUTCRY/MORALE;
COUSIN/FABRIC

PAGE 228
TENANT, IMPEDE,
UNHAND,
PAGODA, URBANE

PAGE 229
SAO PAULO,
ALGIERS,
ANTWERP,
GLASGOW,
LIVERPOOL,
VANCOUVER

PAGE 230
1.

FILL / ZEAL / DOGGY / AIS

2.

```
            F
            A
    Z I G G E D
            O
            L
  S A I L   L
            Y
```

3.
```
              I
  F L A G G E D
  A           O
  Z           L
  Y       I S
```

4.
```
  L
  A       F
  I D O L I Z E
  Y       G
      G A S
```

PAGE 231
ENVELOPE, PAGE;
CLOUD, SHEEP;
CHALK, CREAM;
TEETH, ASPIRIN;
GAUZE, PAPER;
SUGAR, GOOSE

PAGE 232
APOSTLE,
ALCOHOL,
AMNESIA,
ENVELOP

PAGE 233
ANCIENT,
CURTAIL,
UNITARD,
ROTUNDA

DISAVOW

PAGE 234
INVENT, BEHALF,
LAPTOP, CLOTHE,
COBWEB, INTACT,
CHERUB, DOMAIN,
COGNAC, LAYOFF,
GALLOP, DUGOUT

PAGE 235
H: FLASHY,
HEALTH, THRIVE,
CHOSEN

PAGE 236
1–9, 2–8, 3–7,
4–10, 5–12, 6–11

PAGE 237
SOIREE, GLOBAL,
PURSUE, PHOBIA,
MUSEUM, INFAMY,
TALCUM, AVATAR,
PAYDAY, AZALEA

PAGE 238
```
        C
        H
    A L P A C A
        I
```
```
          A
          W
  P A C I F Y
          U
          L
```
```
  W A L R U S
  H
  A
  R
  F
```

PAGE 239
IMBIBE/ROSARY;
TOMBOY/CEMENT;
FROLIC/MYSTIC;
UNUSED/ODDITY

PAGE 240
BEHEST, DEFECT,
UNLOAD, UNHOLY,
DENUDE

PAGE 241
BORING, TRASHY,
BRILLIANT,
FRESH, ORIGINAL,
ENGROSSING

PAGE 242
1.

```
          F
          L
    B A S T E S
          M
  P R O V E D
```

2.
```
  S
  T       O
  A D V E R B
  M
  P
  S E L F
```

3.
```
    S
  R O M P
  A B
  F
  T
  E L V E S
  D
```

4.
```
    F       S
    L   D   E
    A B O V E
    T   R   P
        M   S
```

PAGE 243
MEATBALL,
PIE; APPLE,
TIRE; WHEEL,
MANHOLE;
BUTTON,
MARBLE;
MUSHROOM,
PENNY; RAINBOW,
RING

PAGE 244
DETRACT,
CAPITOL,
SPINACH,
APTNESS

PAGE 245
NARRATE,
CADENCE,
UNCLEAN,
REFRAIN

ATROPHY

PAGE 246
SALOON, COPIER,
BUNION, TIMELY,
REFUTE, ANYWAY,
SAVAGE, TEAPOT,
RARITY, CLEVER,
BITTEN, HIGHER

PAGE 247
A: CARAFE,

RAVAGE, ANEMIA,
FIASCO

PAGE 248
1–10, 2–9, 3–7,
4–11, 5–8, 6–12

PAGE 249
VICTIM, SWATCH,
LEGEND, RETAKE,
BOUGHT,
WOEFUL,
ESCHEW, ARTERY,
ICEBOX, DEVOUR

PAGE 250

```
  M O H A W K
    N
    I
    O
    N
            T
            H
  C A U C U S
            M
            B
  G
  U
  L
  C
  H O B N O B
```

PAGE 251
SESAME/
UNWIND;
UNDONE/
HEALER; SUGARY/
SHROUD;
MAGNET/POETIC

PAGE 252
UPHILL, PAYOUT,
UNPAID, KIMONO,
COHOST

PAGE 253
NUMERAL,
FRACTION,
ALGEBRA,
MIDPOINT,
GEOMETRY,
REMAINDER

PAGE 254

1.

```
      P
O   A R E
V     I
E     Z
I N V I T E
```

2.

```
    I
E V E N
O       Z
T R I V I A
E       P
```

3.

```
      V
R     I
I O N I Z E
V     E
E
T A P
```

4.

```
        V I E
Z I T I
O     I V
N   P A
E   E
    R
```

PAGE 255
BAYONET, PIN;
THORN, STINGER;
NEEDLE, SWORD;
SYRINGE,
CLEAVER;
TOOTHPICK,
MACHETE;
CHEDDAR,
SCISSORS

PAGE 256
RIVALED,
CATFISH,
CHRONIC,
AWESOME

PAGE 257
LEGWORK,
BRISKET,
SPARKLE,
SUNDECK

SUNDOWN

PAGE 258
EGGNOG,
GROWTH,
FATHOM, CICADA,
ASYLUM, BOTTOM,
CLEAVE, PACIFY,
BELONG, FAULTY,
BANISH, PAGODA

PAGE 259
D: INDUCT,
DETACH, FEDORA,
THAWED

PAGE 260
1–9, 2–7, 3–6,
4–10, 5–11, 8–12

PAGE 261
JAGUAR, DUPLEX,
MILDEW, EULOGY,
ELEVEN, UTOPIA,
IMPEDE, SUBMIT,
FLORID, EFFIGY

PAGE 262

```
    G
T I D B I T
    Z
    M
    O
```

```
C A N A R Y
A
N
A
L
```

```
H E C T I C
      O
      P
      A
      Z
```

PAGE 263
GENOME/
THORAX;
HANGUP/
VULGAR; VOYAGE/
WARMTH;
LEGACY/NORMAL

PAGE 264
MANURE, ORNATE,
ALMOND, IMPALE,
FAMOUS

PAGE 265
EUCHRE, RUMMY,
CRIBBAGE,
SOLITAIRE,
BACCARAT,
CANASTA

PAGE 266

1.

```
H U T C H
A     O
N     R
G     N
L E D
R
```

2.

```
      T
C H O R D
      U
A N G L E R
N     H
```

3.

```
    H O T
C   L R
L   A U
HARDEN
N   G
G
```

4.

```
      N
  G   O H
  R   R E
  A   T
L U N C H
  D
```

PAGE 267
COLONEL,
KERNEL; KARAT,
CARET; SIDE,
SIGHED; SOARED,
SWORD; SUEDE,
SWAYED; CHUTE,
SHOOT

PAGE 268
ABSTAIN,
ACREAGE,
GESTURE,
OVERLAP

PAGE 269
GRANOLA,
TENABLE,
APPAREL,
NEUTRAL

FREEDOM

PAGE 270
BAGFUL, DEBTOR,
ENCORE, MARVEL,
LASTLY, OPPOSE,
OFFKEY, LARYNX,
COOKIE, FACIAL,
HUNKER,
MERMEN

PAGE 271
E: ALLEGE,
AMPERE,
MAYHEM, SOLACE

PAGE 272
1–12, 2–9, 3–11,
4–7, 5–8, 6–10

PAGE 273
SOFTEN, EMBODY,
GAUCHE, OUTLAW,
PEYOTE, ENGULF,
MILIEU, BLOWUP,
INDIGO, FELINE

THE AUTHORS

JOE EDLEY

Joe Edley lives for word games. In addition to being a master Bananagrammer, he is also the only three-time National Scrabble Champion (1980, 1992, 2000). Since 1988 he's been the Director of Clubs and Tournaments for the National Scrabble Association. In that role, he has created thousands of word puzzles to entertain the readers of *The Scrabble News*. Joe also writes a syndicated newspaper column, "Scrabblegrams," and teaches at Scrabble events across the country. He lives with his family on Long Island, New York.

BANANAGRAMS

Bananagrams is a family company. Abe Nathanson, along with his daughter Rena and his grandchildren Aaron and Ava, invented the game while spending the summer of 2005 together in Narragansett, Rhode Island. They soon decided—after some encouragement from friends—to try selling it. It debuted at the 2006 London Toy Fair and quickly became an international sensation. The whole family has been actively involved in the growing company. Abe passed away in 2010, but Rena continues to run the company, which has offices in London and Providence, Rhode Island.

Love the Book? Play the Game!

Bananagrams® is the bestselling word game that's fast and fun for the whole family. Using 144 lettered tiles, drawn from a banana-shaped pouch, players race to create their own connecting and intersecting grids. It's simple to play—no pencil, board, or scorepad needed—and a game can be played in as little as 5 minutes. Word lovers of all ages are guaranteed to go bananas for this game!

Visit www.bananagrams.com to learn more.